'WISDOM' INSIGHTS

S.N.Strutt

© S.N.Strutt 2025

Published by S.N.Strutt

The rights of S.N.Strutt to be identified as the author of this work have been asserted by him in accordance with the Copyright, Designs and Patents Act of 1988.
All rights reserved; no part of this publication may be reproduced, stored in a retrieval system, or transmitted in any form or by any means, electronic, mechanical, photocopying, recording or otherwise without the prior written consent of the publisher or a licence permitting copying in the UK issued by the Copyright Licensing Agency Ltd. www.cla.co.uk

ISBN 978-1-78792-101-6

Book design, layout and production management by Into Print
www.intoprint.net
+44 (0)1604 832149

www.insightspublication.com
Editing: L G Strutt

Front cover artwork: Sue Strutt
www.suzannestruttartist/instagram.com
www. suzannestruttartist/facebook.com

Contents

INTRODUCTION. 5
Front cover of this book 7
THE FORMAT OF THIS BOOK 8
CHAPTER 1: HOLY SPIRIT MOTHER. 10
CHAPTER 2: Who Started the Wars? Women or Men? 13
CHAPTER 3: Original Hebrew Language. 18
CHAPTER 4: HIDING THE TRUTH SINCE 364 AD CONCERNING THE HOLY SPIRIT MOTHER 25
CHAPTER 5: SOLOMON TALKED ABOUT THE CONTRAST BETWEEN GOOD AND EVIL 29
CHAPTER 6: WHAT IS THE HOLY SPIRIT HERSELF LIKE? 33
CHAPTER 7: THE WOMB 42
CHAPTER 8: ECCLESIASTICUS - WISDOM OF BEN SIRIACH 46
CHAPTER 9: Writers and Books of the New &Old Testaments. 53
CHAPTER 10: APOCRYPHAL BOOK OF 'WISDOM OF SOLOMON' FROM THE OLD TESTAMENT 57
CHAPTER 11: Holy Spirit Mother. 63
CHAPTER 12: SOPHIA GREEK WORD FOR WISDOM 65
CHAPTER 13: HOLY SPIRIT MOTHER AND THE BIRTH OF A NEW SOUL . . 68
CHAPTER 14: ACTS OF THOMAS & ODES OF SOLOMON 72
CHAPTER 15: THE IMPORTANCE OF MARRIAGE – God Is the One Who Designed Marriage 76
CHAPTER 16: ENDTIMES: LAST 7 YEARS OF HISTORY? *Has it already begun in 2025?*. 82
CHAPTER 17: A CHRISTMAS STORY - 'MOTHER CHRISTMAS' 87
CHAPTER 18: Will There Be Marriage in Heaven? 90
CHAPTER 19: BIBLE MENTIONS OF HOLY SPIRIT 94
CHAPTER 20: HOLY SPIRIT CHANGED FROM FEMALE TO MALE? 100
CHAPTER 21: THE PROPHET OF GOD 102
CHAPTER 22: MY PERSONAL TESTIMONIES ABOUT MEETING THE HOLY SPIRIT MOTHER 104
CHAPTER 23: HEARING FROM GOD. 107
CHAPTER 24: SPIRITUAL HAPPENINGS. 111
CHAPTER 25: LUCIFER AND THE FALLEN ANGELS 112
CHAPTER 26: LOVE. 123
CHAPTER 27: GENESIS 126

CHAPTER 28: BOOK OF ACTS -key verses 135
CHAPTER 29: MILLENIUM -THE GOLDEN AGE. 148
CHAPTER 30: EARLY CHRISTIAN FATHERS & HOLY SPIRIT MOTHER BY OTHER WRITERS 154
APPENDIX I: GENETIC DISINTEGRATION. 162
APPENDIX II: GEO-CENTRIC UNIVERSE 163
APPENDIX III: TIME-FRAME OF 7000 YEARS OF WORLD HISTORY 165
APPENDIX IV: SALVATION 166
APPENDIX V: BOOKS 167

INTRODUCTION

The purpose of this book *'Wisdom' Insights'* is to show some of the best books ever written about 'wisdom' mentioned in the Old Testament and in fact many other places and to show that they all agreed that Wisdom is defined in ancient Hebrew as feminine. Not only in the Hebrew adjective Rua(c)h but a feminine being or Goddess or better said she was known as Mother God.

I will show how it is possible to prove that the Holy Spirit is feminine and that the Holy Spirit and Wisdom in the Old Testament are the same being as Mother God.

We have been told for almost 1700 years that the Holy Spirit is masculine as in the so-called Trinity, but is this true?

In this book we will discuss how countless sources including famous writers, investigators, *Hebrew scholars, theologians and the Early Christians Fathers* all mentioned that the Holy Spirit is Mother God. We notice in the ancient Hebrew writings about Wisdom which is known as the Holy Spirit as in the Wisdom of Solomon, Sirach and many other books. All state that Wisdom is a feminine being.

This book will provide the proof. My hope is simply to inform many of the truth of which they might not be aware.

It is time for everyone to realize the fact that Wisdom is not just a feminine word as in the ancient Hebrew word Ruach, but she is a feminine entity or better said She is Mother God. She is the same as the Holy Spirit. She is the wife of God the Father, and she is also known as the Holy Spirit Mother. Many call her the Divine Feminine.

The Old Testament Jews all referred to Wisdom as a feminine being. We find in doing research that the early Christians referred to the Holy Spirit as Mother' or 'Mother God'.

Let's think logically for a moment. If you asked a small child 'What is necessary for a family? The small child will invariably answer 'A mother'. If the child is that intelligent then why do we believe a fabricated story of all masculine Trinity? This does not make any sense. If Jesus is the Son of God, then who was His mother? The truth is that the Holy Spirit/Wisdom is His Mother.

In this book you will see countless scriptures about the Divine Feminine - Wisdom and the Holy Spirit Mother. She is also known as the Holy Ghost.

When I mention the Divine Feminine, I am talking about the Trinity as having a Mother God – the Holy Spirit Mother. I am certainly not talking about evil demonic goddesses from the negative spirit world.

Mother God is the female goddess above all - as she is next to God the Father and She is Love itself. It is shocking to me how this fact has been deliberately hidden for 1636 years since the Council of Laodicea in 364 AD where the knowledge of the Holy Spirit being feminine was removed along with the books of Enoch.

This topic about the *Holy Spirit Mother* is in my opinion, one of the most interesting and important studies that I have ever done. I have been an avid student studying the Bible, both Old Testament and New Testament for the past 50 + years, as well as many of the Apocryphal books. I have enjoyed studying both the Bible and the Apocrypha very much and they have brought out many secrets that have been hidden from most people until now, such as the Holy Spirit being feminine. The Bible both Old and New Testament as well as many of the Hebrew apocryphal books are, in few words, *miraculous, supernatural & inspiring!* Contrary to what others have stated, I believe that ancient books such as the *Books of Enoch, Jasher, Jubilees, 'Lost Books of Adam and Eve', Testaments of the 12 Patriarchs, & 2nd Esdras* have all revealed many truths and hidden secrets.

Christians believed in the Book of Enoch They also believed in the Holy Spirit Mother,

I have prayed that God would lead, guide and help me by His Holy Spirit to find verses in the Bible that do agree with verses in these ancient texts, & to also explain to the reader some interesting facts.

This is now my twelve book published so far. You can see a list of them at the end of this book.

Front cover of this book

If you are wondering about the front cover of this book, I will try and explain why it is as it is. You might well ask why we made the **Holy Spirit Mother** so very young looking?

In studying about the Holy Spirit Mother, one comes to realize that when she was first created by God the Father for His own companionship and to become Mother God that she was originally *young* as brought out by the various verses that you will find in this book from the old books mentioned.

You could also think 'why is the world so small in the picture? The whole idea of this particular book is to emphasis the Divine Feminine and that the world is completely *safe in her hands* or I should better say in the hands of Mother God who is working for God the Father. God the Father and God the Mother as well as Jesus Christ their Son are more than a match for all of Satan's present evil along with mankind's corruption. God is Love -1 John 4.8

One day in the not-too-distant future Love will prevail and all wars shall cease when Jesus Christ the Saviour returns to lock up Satan and take over the world forever.

The Golden Age of the Millennium will soon start where the influence of the gentle Holy Spirit Mother will be much more profound when scriptures such as Isaiah will finally be fulfilled. In many ways it will become a gentler age than all the ages that preceded it.

Isaiah 11.6 [6] *The wolf also shall dwell with the lamb, and the leopard shall lie down with the kid; and the calf and the young lion and the fatling together; and a little child shall lead them.*

THE FORMAT OF THIS BOOK

i) I have typed a chapter of 'Wisdom Insights', and included in each chapter my commentaries, which are just that: my opinions, speculations and theories as well as inspirations, which are gleaned from much study of the subject matter. Most, if not all of which, could prove to be true, and are written with the express intention to motivate the reader to do a more thorough investigation for him or herself, to prove whether correct or not, as I am sure that some of the ideas, speculations and conjecture will be quite far out there, to some people.

ii) I have also put cross-references to the Bible, and other Apocryphal books where appropriate.

iii) *Details:*

The first *'comment'* in each chapter, will be noted as being '**Comment 1**' & then **C.2,**

C.3, etc. The original Text from the Book of Enoch is in slightly larger text than either the 'comments' or 'Bible verses'. Three different types of writing are used. One for the original text, and another type of writing for my comments, and yet another for the Bible verses.

iv) The longest commentaries and conclusions are in the *'Appendices'* of this book.

v) I have used *italics*, **bold** and underline mostly to try and emphasize important points that are especially related to the Divine Feminine.

vi) I deliberately insist on using the old-time expressions of AD and BC as I am a Christian and do not appreciate the modern expressions of CE and BCE.

'WISDOM' INSIGHTS

CHAPTER 1: HOLY SPIRIT MOTHER

'As for *Wisdom*, what she is, and how she came up, I will tell you and will not hide mysteries from you: but seek her out from the beginning of her *nativity*, and bring the knowledge of her into light and I will not pass over the truth.' 'He created her as the Holy Ghost and saw her'. -**Wisdom of Solomon**

'Wisdom hath been created before all things, and the understanding of prudence from everlasting. The Word of God most high is the fountain of Wisdom; and her ways are everlasting commandments. To whom hath the root of Wisdom been revealed? Or who hath known her wise counsels? Unto whom hath the knowledge of Wisdom been made manifest? and who hath understood her great experience? There is one wise and greatly to be feared, the Lord sitting upon his throne. He created her, and saw her, and numbered her, and poured her out upon all his works.' -**SIRACH**

'When there were no depths, I was brought forth, when there were no fountains abounding with water. Before the mountains were settled, before the hills was, I brought forth: While as yet he had not made the earth, nor the fields, nor the highest part of the dust of the world. When he prepared the heavens, I was there: when he set a compass upon the face of the depth: When he established the clouds above: when he strengthened the fountains of the deep. When he gave to the sea his decree, that the waters should not pass his commandment: when he appointed the foundations of the earth' - **PROVERBS 8.29**

What Is the Gender of The Holy Spirit?

The Traditional Trinity Shows God the Father, God the Son and God the Holy Spirit.

C.1 They are portrayed as either all being masculine or of some sort of ethereal nature that has no gender. This traditional stance could not be further from the truth and the big question is why has the truth been hidden for 1650 years since the council of Laodicea in 364 A.D?

In summary, the facts are that all the early Christian Fathers believed that the Holy Spirit was the female in the Trinity and thus making both God the Father and Jesus the Son the masculine in the Godhead - God the Father is married to Mother God and Jesus is their Son. The Divine Feminine does exist and is in fact Mother God.

C.2 As for Jesus, He has a Bride which are all the believers and saints of all time. I know that for many of us it is a hard concept. How can a man in the flesh be part of a Bride of Christ? Think of that as but a concept or illustration, to explain the close relationship between God the Son and His people.

There is nothing to worry about, as we know we can trust God the Son. He is only loving and pure as well as humble and Holy and only wishes the very best for His Bride.

C.3 Of course, the Bride of Christ is very much tested and tried in this physical life, and she must hold on tight to Jesus her Saviour and His Word in order to survive this physical crazy life as it has become, because of the insane madness of those who currently rule this planet, the satanic Merchants as mentioned in the Book of Revelation: chapters 17-18.

C.4 Everyone needs a mother. From being a tiny baby to being an adult. We all need a mother to comfort us. Why is it that mankind largely tries to get along *without* a mother or comforter?

Without the feminine side mankind becomes very hard-hearted. Of course, when you are an adult man, you desperately need a wife and that has always been God's perfect plan. Without the male and female there is no future for humankind – we need babies and children. Unfortunately, the West is going the direction of next to no children anymore. More than half of women in the West no longer get married until 30 or older. Something is wrong!

Mother and Baby:

Today I saw a lovely sight. I had entered a popular café to notice in the middle of the café a young woman holding up her 4–6-month baby boy in front of her. She was cuddling and kissing him, and she was ecstatic with love for her baby boy, and he was just so happy to receive so much love and affection from his sweet young mum. I had the impression that she was so happy because at some time or other things had not been so easy for her or the baby or even for both of them. Now she was able to fully enjoy her baby, and he was just tickled pink! The Joy of motherhood at its best! I would wish that many more women could enjoy the beauty of motherhood.

The Holy Spirit Mother has been trying to encourage women for thousands of years to have their babies and to treat them lovingly.

This world is seriously lacking the fruits of the Spirit of God as the world has become so hard-hearted in their interactions with each other and so many people today have no love lost for each other. Many are without natural affection.

Galatians 5.22-23 But the fruit of the Spirit is love, joy, peace, longsuffering, gentleness, goodness, faith, Meekness, temperance: against such there is no law.

C.5 Why has the feminine side of things throughout history been side-lined?

Hiding the Truth Concerning the Holy Spirit Mother Since 364 AD. It is a shocking reality that we have all been hood-winked by the religious authorities for almost 1700 years or since 364 AD at the council of Laodicea when a papal edict declared that certain things that the Christian churches had accepted as doctrine up until that time would no longer be accepted. In fact, the punishment for such so-called blasphemy or continuing to talk about these topics and books became punishable by death or burning at the stake for heresy against the church. I will list some of the books and also mention the early Christian writers and church Fathers who all believed that the Holy Spirit is female.

C.6 The books of Enoch were banned in 364 A.D. at the threat of being burned alive at the stake. The Holy Spirit was changed from female to male entity and incorporated into the all-masculine Trinity.

How did this happen? The original text was in Hebrew and then translated into Greek and then into Latin. The word for Holy Spirit in Hebrew is Ruach which is a feminine word. It was translated into Greek as pneuma which is a neutral word and then into Latin spiritus which is a masculine word. Somehow the femininity of the Holy Spirit was lost. Either accidentally or deliberately and on purpose. This has done so much damage to humanity in so many ways. According to the writer Ally Kateusz and her amazing book 'Finding Holy Spirit Mother' (c. 2008) 85% of original Christian writings from the times of the Early Christian Fathers have been lost altogether. They were burned by the Catholic church at different times throughout its long history. Many of those writings were burned because they stated that the Holy Spirit is female. Other writings were burned because they mentioned the Books of Enoch. The Early Catholic church and its last vestiges of the old Roman empire wanted to make sure that it had total demonic control of the Christian churches through fear of Papal edict. One could be burned at the stake for going against Rome. The Holy Roman empire actually just continued from the old Roman Empire for another 1000 years from 500 AD with the collapse of dictatorial Roman Caesars transferring the power to the Catholic church and its Popes, but to a different form. Religious control and then political control. The Catholic church is one of the richest religions in the world with thousands of properties and some of the best pieces of art in the world. The worth of the Vatican and its underground treasures is unknown. Total worth of the Catholic church world-wide is in the trillions.

C.7 Rich churches remind me of what Jesus said about the Laodicean church in Revelation chapter 3.

Revelation 3.13-19 He that hath an ear, let him hear what the Spirit saith unto the churches.

And unto the angel of the church of the Laodiceans write; These things saith the Amen, the faithful and true witness, the beginning of the creation of God; I know thy works, that thou art neither cold nor hot: I would thou wert cold or hot. So then because thou art lukewarm, and neither cold nor hot, I will spue thee out of my mouth.

"Because thou sayest, I am rich, and increased with goods, and have need of nothing; and knowest not that thou art wretched, and miserable, and poor, and blind, and naked: "I counsel thee to buy of me gold tried in the fire, that thou mayest be rich; and white raiment, that thou mayest be clothed, and *that* the shame of thy nakedness do not appear; and anoint thine eyes with eye salve, that thou mayest see.

As many as I love, I rebuke and chasten: be zealous therefore, and repent.

CHAPTER 2: Who Started the Wars? Women or Men?

C.1 Notice in history; it has not been the women who started all the wars and endless destruction of human beings. It is the rich men of power, who are led by demons who bring wars upon mankind.

Revelation 6.15 "And the kings of the earth, and the great men, and the rich men, and the chief captains, and the mighty men.

THE FEMININE SIDE: The gentler nature or the feminine side tends to nurture and protect human beings as you see many female nurses in warzones nurturing and protecting or trying to protect others while even risking their own lives in the process.

1 Thessalonians 2.7 But we were *gentle* among you, even as a nurse cherishes her children.

C.2 It is very important to see the spiritual side of things. It is this very nature of the feminine side that Satan hates and does his best to try and destroy. This is why in recent modern times 'so-called', that people are no longer getting married or having babies and families. God's very first commandment to the very first man and woman on the planet was to 'be fruitful and multiply'.

C.3 In the following verse God was talking to man and all the creations that he had just created:

Genesis 1.22 'And God blessed them, saying, 'Be fruitful, and multiply, and fill the waters in the seas, and let fowl multiply in the earth'.

C.4 In this verse God was talking to Noah and his family after the Great Flood:

Genesis 9.7 'And you, be ye fruitful, and multiply; bring forth abundantly in the earth, and multiply therein.'

C.5 Evil Spirits: The evil spirits or devils and demons are leading mankind astray into all kinds of arrogance, pride, violence and perversions. 'Anything goes' as there is no God they say, and therefore no rules - just do what you want is the slogan of devils as there is no accountability.

Proverbs 8:13 The fear of the LORD is to hate evil: pride, and arrogancy, and the evil way, and the froward mouth, do I hate.

C.6 THERE IS A PERFECT DESCRIPTION OF THE HOLY SPIRIT MOTHER OR DIVINE FEMININE IN THE BOOK OF PROVERBS IN THE BIBLE:

Proverbs 8

Doth not wisdom cry? And understanding put forth her voice?

She stands in the top of high places, by the way in the places of the paths.

She cries at the gates, at the entry of the city, at the coming in at the doors.

Unto you, O men, I call; and my voice is to the sons of man.

Receive my instruction, and not silver, and knowledge rather than choice gold.

For wisdom is better than rubies; and all the things that may be desired are not to be compared to it.

I wisdom dwell with prudence and find out knowledge of witty inventions.

C.7 It seems to me that Prudence is also personified as a spirit being or an archangel that accompanies the Holy Spirit Mother and is possibly her protector and watches out for her safety. Angelic security guard perhaps? Even God the Father has his own security force. The spirit world or heaven is highly organized with God's archangels in control. Our Father God and the Holy Spirit Mother along with their Son Jesus have been setting the hierarchy of heaven up by testing the angels of God. (Check 2nd Enoch about Wisdom living with the angels or amongst them)

Definition of *prudence:* caution or circumspection as to danger or risk. Another definition is knowing 'when is the exact right time to do something'.

C.8 The Holy Spirit likes to create and thus 'find out knowledge of witty inventions' and thus She must have others around her taking care of other important matters. This would suggest that God the Father and God the Mother could now be involved in creating other spheres and universes, since this particular creation of the earth is wearing out because of sin and disobedience. The Bible tells us that at the end of the Millennium God will burn the whole surface of the planet.

More on Proverbs 8.15-35

C.9 The Holy Spirit Mother was predicting in the time of Solomon how the ideal should be. Solomon was one of the few good kings of Israel, well at least for most of his life.

^{15}By me kings reign, and princes decree justice.

C.10 In order for kings to rule wisely they would have to listen to the Holy Spirit and take time with God. Not as in modern times, when the kings and rulers follow Satan and his Materialism because they have been deceived.

^{16}By me princes rule, and nobles, even all the judges of the earth.

C.11 Unfortunately not as this present world is. It will be when Christ returns the 2nd time.

^{17}'I love them that love me; and those that seek me early shall find me.'

C.12 'Seek me early'. This could mean 'early in life' when you are a small child or 'early in the morning'. N.B When you pray and talk to Jesus and the Holy Spirit early in the morning you will have protection all day long.

In the following Bible verses from Proverbs the Holy Spirit or Wisdom is

talking about herself:

¹⁸Riches and honour are with me; yea, durable riches and righteousness.

¹⁹My fruit is better than gold, yea, than fine gold; and my revenue than choice silver.

²⁰I lead in the way of righteousness, in the midst of the paths of judgment:

²¹That I may cause those that love me to inherit substance; and I will fill their treasures.

²²The Lord possessed me in the beginning of his way, before his works of old.

²³I was set up from everlasting, from the beginning, or ever the earth was.

²⁴When there were no depths, I was brought forth; when there were no fountains abounding with water.

²⁵ Before the mountains were settled, before the hills was I brought forth:

²⁶ While as yet he had not made the earth, nor the fields, nor the highest part of the dust of the world.

²⁷ When he prepared the heavens, I was there: when he set a compass upon the face of the depth:

²⁸ When he established the clouds above: when he strengthened the fountains of the deep:

²⁹ When he gave to the sea his decree, that the waters should not pass his commandment: when he appointed the foundations of the earth:

³⁰ Then I was by him, as one brought up with him: and I was daily his delight, rejoicing always before him;

³¹ Rejoicing in the habitable part of his earth; and my delights were with the sons of men.

³² Now therefore hearken unto me, O ye children: for blessed are they that keep my ways.

³³ Hear instruction, and be wise, and refuse it not.

³⁴ Blessed is the man that heareth me, watching daily at my gates, waiting at the posts of my doors.

³⁵ For whoso finds me (Wisdom) finds life and shall obtain favour of the Lord.

C.13 Wisdom is a feminine word (Ruah in ancient Hebrew) and is equated with the Holy Spirit who is also female.

C.14 Wisdom states that she sends forth her maidens to help mankind and that her delights are with the sons of men. She also states that She herself is

'Daily His delights' talking about God the Father. What do you suppose that means. Does not a husband delight in his beautiful wife who gives him much pleasure? Of course, on an eternal level involving God the Father and God the Holy Spirit Mother it is on a much better and eternal scale than what goes on in the physical life or let's say more complete. The woman, in this case the Holy Spirit Mother, is a big delight to God the Father because as pointed out so well in the 2nd book of Enoch for those with 'eyes to see' and 'ears to hear' because she has a lot to do with the Creation - especially of the feminine side of things.

Proverbs 9 describes WISDOM

[1] Wisdom hath built her house, she hath hewn out her seven pillars:

[2] She hath killed her beasts; she hath mingled her wine; she hath also furnished her table.

[3] She hath sent forth her maidens: she cries upon the highest places of the city.

C.15 What house was Wisdom or Holy Spirit Mother building? What are the 7 pillars to her house? That sounds like a magnificent palace with 7 tall pillars What beasts has She killed? What do you think that we would eat at the marriage supper of the Lamb of God? What wine has She mingled? I am sure that God has prepared the very best wine for the Marriage Feast of the Lamb Who are her maidens? The Holy Spirits maidens could be the female Virtues. What table was She furnishing? Where are the highest places of the city?

C.16 The Holy Spirit who is Wisdom herself was sent by God to teach those who will listen about the future *'Wedding Feast of the Lamb'* or the *Marriage of the saints* of all time to *Jesus Christ our Saviour.*

Matthew 26:29 (Jesus) But I say unto you, I will not drink henceforth of this **fruit of the vine**,(wine) until that day when I drink it new with you in my Father's kingdom.

John 14.2-3

[2] In my Father's house are many mansions: if it were not so, I would have told you. I go to prepare a place for you..

[3] And if I go and prepare a place for you, I will come again, and receive you unto myself; that where I am, there ye may be also.

Revelation 19.7-9

[7] Let us be glad and rejoice, and give honour to him: for the marriage of the Lamb is come, and his wife hath made herself ready.

[8] And to her was granted that she should be arrayed in fine linen, clean and white: for the fine linen is the righteousness of saints.

[9] And he saith unto me, Write, Blessed *are* they which are called unto the marriage supper of the Lamb. And he saith unto me, These are the true sayings of God.

Proverbs 9.4-5,10-11

[4] Whoso is simple, let him turn in hither: as for him that wants understanding, she saith to him,

[5] Come, eat of my bread, and drink of the wine which I have mingled.

[10] The fear of the Lord is the beginning of wisdom: and the knowledge of the holy is understanding.

[11] For by me thy days shall be multiplied, and the years of thy life shall be increased.

C.17 In the Book of Proverbs we see some examples of *Wisdom* being described as feminine in nature. We find examples in the New Testament Bible of the Holy Spirit also being described as feminine.

C.18 The *Comforter* mentioned by Jesus in the New Testament also is described as feminine and of having a feminine role as Comforter. The *Holy Spirit, Wisdom* and the *Comforter* are all one and the same feminine being of *Mother God* who is the feminine in the so-called Trinity. As they say there are no babies without the mother or Mother.

C.19 Another description of the feminine is the constant reference to '*the Womb of the Earth'* as in 2 Esdras.

2 Esdras 5:48: Then said he unto me, 'Even so have I given the *womb of the earth* to those that be sown in it in their times'.

C.20 In talking about the 'womb of the earth' is God just mentioning through his prophet Esra the physical earth or even more importantly is He talking about the birth of immortal souls as through the Holy Spirit Mother.

CHAPTER 3: Original Hebrew Language

C.1 What would the scriptures look like if the true feminine Holy Spirit were properly included?

COMFORTER - I have transformed the following Bible verses about the Comforter into their 'original form' of the Holy Spirit Mother - in both Greek and Hebrew as in the time of Jesus and His disciples:

John 14.26- But the Comforter, which is the Holy Ghost, whom the Father will send in my name, She shall teach you all things, and bring all things to your remembrance, whatsoever I have said unto you.

John 15.26 But when the Comforter is come, whom I will send unto you from the Father, even the Spirit of truth, which proceeds from the Father, She shall testify of me:

John 16.13- Howbeit when *She*, the Spirit of truth, is come, She will guide you into all truth: for She shall not speak of Herself; but whatsoever She shall hear, that shall She speak: and *She* will shew you things to come.

John 16.7 - Nevertheless I tell you the truth; It is expedient for you that I go away: for if I go not away, the Comforter will not come unto you; but if I depart, I will send Her unto you.

John 14.16 - And I will pray the Father, and he shall give you another Comforter, that She may abide with you for ever;

John 14.17- Even the Spirit of truth; whom the world cannot receive, because it sees Her not, neither knows Her not: but ye know Her; for She dwelleth with you, and shall be in you.

John 7.39 (But this spake he of the Spirit Mother, which they that believe on him should receive: for the Holy Ghost was not yet given; because that Jesus was not yet glorified.)

Romans 8.1-39 There is therefore now no condemnation to them which are in Christ Jesus, who walk not after the flesh, but after the Spirit of God the Mother.

John 14.16-17 And I will pray the Father, and he shall give you another Comforter, that *she* may abide with you for ever;

John 4.24 God the Mother is a Spirit: and they that worship her must worship her in spirit and in truth.

Acts 2.3-4 And there appeared unto them cloven tongues like as of fire, and it sat upon each of them.

Acts 2.33 - Therefore being by the right hand of God exalted, and having received of the Father the promise of the Holy Ghost Mother, he hath shed forth this, which ye now see and hear.

John 3.34 - For he whom God hath sent speaks the words of God: for God giveth not the Spirit Mother by measure unto him.

Ephesians 4.30 - And grieve not the Holy Spirit or Mother of God, whereby ye are sealed unto the day of redemption. The woman makes the perfect balance for the man just as the Holy Spirit Mother makes the perfect balance to God the Father.

C.2 I believe that this explains clearly why Jesus stated 'Whatsoever word a man speaks against the Son of Man can be forgiven, but whatever is spoken against the Holy Spirit Mother will not be forgiven him in this world or the next.

C.3 Here are just a few verses from the KJV of the Bible mentioning the Spirit of God, which is really talking about Holy Spirit Mother and her caring for us as her children as well as protecting us and instructing us in the ways of the Lord.

C.4 NB All the Old Hebrew books mention the Spirit of God and denote her as being a feminine being. She is known as Ruach, the Spirit of God and Wisdom as in the Proverbs of Solomon. Wisdom of Solomon, Ecclesiasticus and many other ancient Hebrew Apocryphal books.

Romans 8.16 The Spirit itself bears witness with our spirit, that we are the children of God:

C.5 You can see in this verse that the Holy Spirit is in close communion with us her children.

1 Corinthians 2.10 But God hath revealed them unto us by his Spirit: for the Spirit searches all things, yea, the deep things of God.

C.6 Holy Spirit Mother goes out of her way to find Gods position on any given topic and she shows it to us, her children.

C.7 There are those who claim to be Christians, but they have not the Spirit of God which is a loving and caring Spirit and certainly not hateful, negative and accusing others - as many religionists are like the Pharisees in Jesus time.

Romans 8.9 But ye are not in the flesh, but in the Spirit, if so be that the Spirit of God dwell in you. Now if any man have not the Spirit of Christ, he is none of his.

C.8 It is important to receive Jesus as our Saviour and to pray for the anointing of the Holy Spirit Mother who will give us the power and anointing to be a witness for God - to give us enough love to sacrifice our owns lives to live for Christ as one of His disciples preaching the gospel of Salvation.

1 Corinthians 2.2 Now we have received, not the spirit of the world, but the *Spirit Mother* which is of God; that we might know the things that are freely given to us of God.

C.9 The secret is that you must have the Spirit of Mother God to know the truth in full, as it is given from heaven.

1 John 4.6 We are of God: he that knows God heareth us; he that is not of God heareth not us. Hereby know we the spirit of truth, and the spirit of error.

C.10 This is an accurate statement just by observation. Some people will listen to our witness of Salvation through the Messiah Jesus Christ and yet others refuse to want to know.

Ezekial 11.24 Afterwards the spirit took me up, and brought me in a vision by the Spirit of God into Chaldea, to them of the captivity. So, the vision that I had seen went up from me.

C.11 It is indeed Spirit of Mother God who takes us up to see visions or dream dreams of heaven.

1 Corinthians 2.11 For what man knows the things of a man, save the spirit of man which is in him? Even so the things of God knows no man, but the Spirit of God.

C.12 It is so important to be praying about everything we do and thus be led by the Spirit of Mother God. She can tell us things about a situation before it even happens. Afterall, there is no time in the spirit world.

John 4.24 God is a *Spirit*: and they that worship him must worship him in spirit and in truth.

C.13 What is this saying? If we want to worship God, then we do it through the Truth. Jesus is the truth according to John.

John 14.6 'I am the way the truth and life, no man cometh unto the Father but be Me. Neither is there salvation in any other. For there is no other name under heaven given among men whereby we must be saved.

C.14 The Spirit of God points to the way of Salvation and She is both loving and tender-hearted.

Isaiah 11.2 .

C.15 This verse clearly shows that the Holy Spirit Mother is taking care of her Son the Messiah.

John 3.34 For he whom God hath sent speak the words of God: for God giveth not the Spirit by measure unto him.

C.16 When you have the Spirit of Mother God there is 'no limit' to what might be given to you by the Spirit of God. Think of how much was given to Moses and all that was given to Jesus.

Matthew 12.28 But if I cast out devils by the Spirit of God, then the kingdom of God is come unto you.

C.17 Amazing how that evil spirits in people can be cast out through God's Holy Spirit. This also applies to haunted or disturbed buildings.

Ezekiel 1.20 Whithersoever the spirit was to go, they went, thither was their spirit to go; and the wheels were lifted up over against them: for the spirit of the living creature was in the wheels.

C.18 The Spirit of God was in the wheels. For the spirit of the living creatures was in the wheels. How can wheels be alive being at least, seemingly mechanical, but not physical of course.? Very strange description. I suppose this description is very strange for us humans as an earthly comparison would be if a mechanical device on earth like a car was *alive* like the Herbie-car in the old movie.

1 Corinthians 6.20 For ye are bought with a price: therefore glorify God in your body, and in your spirit, which are God's.

C.19 Jesus is the One who paid the price for our Salvation and therefore we owe it to God to behave ourselves in a godly manner.

1 Corinthians 3.16 Know ye not that ye are the temple of God, and that the Spirit of God dwelleth in you?

C.20 A temple is a building, that when empty, is able to contain other things like people. God wants us to invite the Spirit of God to dwell in us. If Holy Spirit Mother lives within us, then we need to make our building acceptable for her and inviting through our humility and love towards Jesus.

Psalm 51.10 Create in me a clean heart, O God; and renew a right spirit within me.

C.21 Cause me to have a humble and contrite heart, O God; renew my spirit by your Holy Spirit.

Romans 8.14 For as many as are led by the Spirit of God, they are the sons of God.

C.22 Led by Holy Spirit Mother as we are her sons and desire to please her our Mother.

Hebrews 9.14 How much more shall the blood of Christ, who through the eternal Spirit offered himself without spot to God, purge your conscience from dead works to serve the living God?

C.23 This shows that Jesus collaborated very much with His Mother - Holy Spirit Mother to give his life as a sacrifice to God for the sins of the world.

Galatians 5.25 If we live in the Spirit, let us also walk in the Spirit.

C.24 If we have the Holy Ghost or Holy Spirit then we should use her power in order to be a witness for Jesus and His love and Salvation.

Ephesians 2.22 In whom ye also are built together for an habitation of God through the Spirit.

C.25 The Holy Spirit Mother is the One who builds the true church of God through all the members.

2 Tim 3.5,7 Having a form of godliness but denying the power thereof: from such turn away., Ever learning, and never able to come to the knowledge of the truth.

C.26 Most of the religious people of the world have a 'form of godliness' but they deny the power of the Holy Ghost, as the scripture states:' Ever learning and never coming to the knowledge of the truth. Jesus stated, 'I am the Way the Truth and the Life, no man cometh unto the Father but by Me'. We cannot come to God without Jesus the Saviour and that is the mistake that most religions make.

C.27 Here are some Bible verses on the Holy Ghost, which is the same as the Holy Spirit: We could call her Holy Ghost Mother as well as Holy Spirit Mother or Wisdom = Sophia (Greek) The true feminine representative of God.

John 14.26 But the Comforter, which is the Holy Ghost, whom the Father will send in my name, She (not He) shall teach you all things, and bring all things to your remembrance, whatsoever I have said unto you.

C.28 The Comforter acts like a mother because She is a Mother. Like a mother she comforts her children and teaches them the ways of righteousness as taught by Jesus Christ the Messiah - Her Son.

Acts 2.38 Then Peter said unto them, Repent, and be baptized every one of you in the name of Jesus Christ for the remission of sins, and ye shall receive the gift of the Holy Ghost.

C.29 'Repent and be baptized' in essence means 'rend your heart' and not your garment and cry out to God for the forgiveness of all your sins. Getting baptized is not a religious ceremony but simply asking Jesus into your heart that you might be saved eternally. Receiving the Holy Ghost is normally a separate action from getting saved and She the Holy Spirit Mother is for the anointing to empower a person to witness about Christ being the Saviour. It is also to empower one to pray for others to also receive Jesus into their hearts as their Saviour. - John 3.36 He that believe on the Son has eternal life.

John 1.32-34 And John bare record, saying, I saw the Spirit descending from heaven like a dove, and it abode upon him. And I knew him not: but he that sent me to baptize with water, the same said unto me, upon whom thou shalt see the Spirit descending, and remaining on him, the same is he which baptizes with the Holy Ghost. And I saw, and bare record that this is the Son of God.

C.30 Here we see Jesus baptised through the Holy Ghost His Mother as She brings rebirth to souls.

Titus 3.5 Not by works of righteousness which we have done, but according to his mercy he saved us, by the washing of regeneration, and renewing of the Holy Ghost.

C.31 How does the baptism of the Holy Spirit renew us. The difference between getting saved and getting the anointing of the Holy Spirit. Many people pray to receive Jesus but fail to get the anointing of the Holy Spirit who empowers God's children to witness and tell others about Jesus and Salvation. However, the Spirit of God is not given to everyone but unto those who obey God and do what Jesus commanded to 'Go into all the world and preach the Gospel of Salvation through Jesus Christ unto every creature.'.

Acts 5.32 And we are his witnesses of these things; and so is also the Holy Ghost, whom God hath given to them that obey him.

C.32 If we want to have the full power of the Holy Ghost then we need to obey what God is telling us to do at any given moment. God tries to send us messages by His Holy Spirit Mother but it all depends if we listen to them and follow through on those messages.

Acts 1.8 But ye shall receive power, after that the Holy Ghost is come upon you: and ye shall be witnesses unto me both in Jerusalem, and in all Judaea, and in Samaria, and unto the uttermost part of the earth.

C.33 We receive the power to tell others about Jesus by praying with them to receive the Lord Jesus into their hearts and to be filled with His Holy Spirit. The Holy Spirit Mother gives God's disciples the power and anointing to be bold and stand up for Jesus.

Romans 8.26-27 Likewise the Spirit also helps our infirmities: for we know not what we should pray for as we ought: but the Spirit itself maketh intercession for us with groanings which cannot be uttered.

C.34 Speaking in tongues which cannot be uttered - the language of heaven which few understand, but God does.

John 16.13 Howbeit when She, the Spirit of truth, is come, She will guide you into all truth: for She shall not speak of herself; but whatsoever She shall hear, that shall She speak: and She will shew you things to come.

C.35 Notice that I have put 'She' instead of the traditional 'he', as She was the original in the Hebrew language.

Ephesians 4.30 And grieve not the holy Spirit of God, whereby ye are sealed unto the day of redemption.

C.36 Jesus warned us not to grieve the Spirit of God as that would not be forgiven in this world or the next.

John 8.32 And ye shall know the truth, and the truth shall make you free.

C.37 When you know Jesus in person as well as the truth about His Holy Spirit Mother, it sets you free from all of Satan's lies.

John 3.5 Jesus answered, Verily, verily, I say unto thee, 'Except a man be born of water and of the Spirit, he cannot enter into the kingdom of God.'

C.38 The Holy Spirit Mother being female is the one who gives birth to all the souls that get saved just like a physical baby in the womb of water a spiritual baby is born by the Holy Spirit Mother.

1 Corinthians 3.16-17 Know ye not that ye are the temple of God, and that the Spirit of God dwelleth in you?

C.39 We are the temple of God when God's Spirit abides in us.

Romans 15.13 Now the God of hope fill you with all joy and peace in believing, that ye may abound in hope, through the power of the Holy Ghost.

C.40 The Holy Ghost being the same as the Holy Spirit Mother fills us with joy and peace because of our faith in Jesus Her Son, as we believe in simple salvation by grace.

Luke 1.35 And the angel answered and said unto her, The Holy Ghost shall come upon thee, and the power of the Highest shall overshadow thee: therefore also that holy thing which shall be born of thee shall be called the Son of God.

C.41 This is an amazing verse which is clearly showing the involvement of both God the Father and the Holy Spirit Mother to create their Son Jesus on earth through the body of Mary wife of Joseph.

CHAPTER 4: HIDING THE TRUTH SINCE 364 AD CONCERNING THE HOLY SPIRIT MOTHER

Comment No 1. It is a shocking reality that we have all been hood-winked by the religious authorities for almost 1700 years or since 364 AD at the Catholic church council of Laodicea, when a papal edict declared that certain things that the Christian churches had accepted as doctrine up until that time would no longer be accepted. In fact the punishment of continuing to talk about these topics and books became punishable by death or burning at the stake for heresy against the church. I will list some of the books and mention the early Christian writers and church Fathers who all believed that the Holy Spirit is female.

C.2 The books of Enoch were banned in 364 AD at the threat of being burned alive at the stake.

C.3 The Holy Spirit was changed from a female to male entity and incorporated into the all-masculine Trinity. How did this happen? The original text was in Hebrew and then translated into Greek and then into Latin. The word for Holy Spirit in Hebrew is Ruach which is a feminine word. It was translated into Greek as pneuma which is a neutral word and then into Latin spiritus which is a masculine word. Somehow the femininity of the Holy Spirit was lost. Either accidentally or deliberately and on purpose. This has done so much damage to humanity in so many ways.

C.4 Ever since that time the sexes have been segregated especially amongst the very religious and it has born very bad fruit along the levels of the demonic and as those things mentioned in the 2nd Book of Enoch.

EVIL CAUSED BY GETTING RID OF THE DIVINE FEMININE IN HISTORY

C.5 Here we can read about what God thought about those who lift up an 'all-male side' as in the Trinity portrayed by the Catholic church in 364 AD of things and what that leads to. See my book 'Secrets of Enoch Insights': 2nd Enoch 10.1-3.

1 'AND those two men (angels) led me upon to the Northern side, and showed me there a very terrible place, and there were all manner of tortures in that place: cruel darkness and unillumined gloom, and there is no light there, but murky fire constantly flames aloft, and there is a fiery river coming forth, and that whole place is everywhere fire, and everywhere there is frost and ice, thirst and shivering, while the bonds are very cruel, and the angels fearful and merciless, bearing angry weapons, merciless torture, and I said;

2 'Woe, woe, how very terrible is this place.

3 And those men (angels) said to me: This place, O Enoch, is prepared for those who dishonour God, who on earth practise sin against nature, which is child-corruption after the sodomite fashion, magic-making, enchantments and devilish witchcrafts, and who boast of their wicked deeds, stealing, lies, calumnies*, envy, rancour, fornication, murder, and who, accursed, steal the souls of men, who, seeing the poor take away their goods and themselves

wax rich, injuring them for other men's goods; who being able to satisfy the empty, made the hungering to die; being able to clothe, stripped the naked; and who knew not their creator, and bowed down to soulless (sc. lifeless) gods, who cannot see nor hear, vain gods, who also built hewn images and bow down to unclean handiwork, for all these is prepared this place amongst these, for eternal inheritance.'

C.6 I personally attended boarding schools from the age of 8-18 years old. I think of the all-boy boarding schools throughout the many centuries of the so-called elite kings and leaders of the church hierarchy with the plan to deliberately de-femininize the church, not to mention the Catholic church which has totally defeminized the church with the exception of Mary the physical mother of Jesus, which is a reflection of His spiritual Mother the Holy Spirit Mother. The Roman empire was still in power until about 500 AD when it became the Holy Roman Empire for the next 1000 years until the Reformation in 1500 AD.

C.7 Look at the so-called elite, the kind of people that it produced here in the UK and its fellow royals in Europe? Why do they all almost without exception follow demonic organizations such as the masons and the illuminati? Why are the leaders of this world deviant in so many ways? So many perverts! The truth is that it is demonic and satanic.

C.8 It is also satanic to take away the woman or the female from Creation. The truth is that the elite follow the ways of the Fallen angels and their sons the Giants of pre-flood times who after they died in pre-flood times became the disembodied spirits of the giants or better known as the demons according to the Hebrew Book of Jubilees.

C.9 The Fallen angels are known as the devils and their sons as the demons. In Pre-Flood times the Fallen angels made the horrendous crime of stealing the beautiful women on the earth away from their husbands. The women according to Genesis 6 and Enoch 6, Jubilees 5 and Jasher 4 gave birth to giants.

C.10 Unfortunately for the giants apparently there were no female giants, so they eventually became only interested in other male giants. Why were there no female giants? Now that is a very good question, which I have covered in chapter 25 of this book.

C.11 Well, it is all about realizing that there is a female in the so-called Trinity and without involving her in creation the Fallen angels could only have sons with the women on the earth. That is my take on it.

C.12 This is where the perverted spirits began. When the physical giants died, they went down to the negative spirit world and according to the Book of Jubilees they came back as the disembodied spirits of the Giants or what we call demons today.

C.13 That is when sicknesses started just after the Great Flood according to the Book of Jubilees. These entities are not to be played around with as they are very destructive and harmful. They cause sickness and diseases of all types.

WHAT HAS BEEN THE REASON FOR HIDING THE FACTS ABOUT THE HOLY SPIRIT BEING FEMALE?

C.14 This story goes back to the beginning of time. Once upon a time God the Father, who is Love, according to the Bible was all alone and yes, He was lonely. (Ref. 2nd Enoch)

C.15 Notice how God has created us humans just like Himself. We long to find real love as we are created in His image. As humans both male and female we go through different stages in growing up. Our longings for love change as we grow up.

C.16 I can only speak for myself in stating that as I grew up being in all-boys boarding schools, I longed for female company. I didn't' have a proper relationship with a woman until I was around 18 years old. I had girlfriends when I was younger. I even had a girlfriend when I was 5 years old. When I was just 5-years old we held hands only.

The pull between male and female can be very strong when you are young.

I think that is a reflection of how it must have been for God the Father Himself. God created the perfect mate and wife for the first creation or man - Adam. How did God the Father know how to create the perfect woman for Adam?

C.17 Well, I think it becomes very clear that there had to be some feminine influence in the creation of Eve. Women are not just different from us men sexually and in body. Every cell in their body cries out that they are female. The same is true about their spirits. Women are fascinating and they know they are, and many make use of that fact.

C.18 Each generation has its things to learn about life. Wisdom is one of the things often left until people get older in general, as they have more time to think about deeper things.

GOD THE FATHER, GOD THE MOTHER, AND GOD THE SON

C.19 To bring our minds back into perspective as is often stated 'If you imagine that God the Father is a like a great iceberg. Most of which is hidden under the sea of eternity. Jesus the Son is like the part of the iceberg that one can see above the surface of the sea and God the Father the part under the ocean of eternity. It is also stated that Jesus was the beginning of the Creation of God. It also states that 'There are three that agree together in heaven.

1 John 5:7 The Father, the Son and the Holy Ghost' and these three are one.

When one realizes that the Holy Spirit is the female in the family, and also the Mother, then everything else in life makes so much more sense.

1 John 4.8 He that loveth not knows not God; for God is love.

C.20 In the beginning, God being an eternal being, omniscient, all powerful, God the Father decided that He had to create an eternal being like unto Himself and yet totally different.

The story goes something like this. Once upon a time there was God Almighty who was all by Himself. (Please bear with me as it is very difficult to define things in the realm of time itself.)

In simple terms God felt alone and in the need for an equal partner and yet totally different than Himself. So, He invented the Holy Spirit Mother to be His loving companion who would have the eternal powers to create and develop using her very imaginative and feminine mind as women wonderfully do, to make their families beautiful and their children well cared for. It is stated that in a marital relationship where the woman is pregnant that the man thinks of a few things concerning her but that the budding mother is thinking and planning twenty things in preparation for her offspring.

God the Father had the protector's role and often the Holy Spirit Mother along with Her Son Jesus had a creating role of the physical realm, as in the Book of Genesis and as evidenced by the 'Spirit of God was upon the water'.

Genesis 1.2 And the earth was without form, and void; and darkness was upon the face of the deep. And the **Spirit of God** moved upon the face of the waters.

C.21 Genesis 1.2 It should read 'Spirit of Mother God'

CHAPTER 5: SOLOMON TALKED ABOUT THE CONTRAST BETWEEN GOOD AND EVIL

C.1 In the Proverbs we see two very interesting characters:

WISDOM clearly shown as feminine

UNRIGHTEOUSNESS also feminine and portrayed as a whorish woman.

In 'The 1st Book of Enoch' it also mentions these two woman or feminine powers 1) Wisdom 2) Unrighteousness - who is more like the Great Whore described in Revelation 17-18.

The '2nd' Book of Enoch mentions what looks like a good feminine entity and an evil or dark female entity at the time of Pre-Creation before God had even created the physical realm. Both women, or female entities were giving birth to life. The first giving birth to creations of Light and the 2nd giving birth to things of Darkness.

C.2 Here is some of the original text, which is somewhat confusing as it is made out to be a pregnant male entity which is obviously erroneous as only the female gets pregnant.

Here is the account of the 1st good entity of LIGHT:-

'SECRETS OF ENOCH CHAPTER 25

'I *(God the Father) commanded in the very lowest parts, that visible things should come down from invisible, and Adoil came down very great, and I beheld him, and lo! he had a belly of great light.*

2 And I said to him: 'Become undone, Adoil, and let the visible come out of thee.'

3 And he came undone, and a great light came out. And I was in the midst of the great light, and as there is born light from light, there came forth a great age, and showed all creation, which I had thought to create.

C.3 Here is the account of the 2ND evil entity of Darkness: - Here is some of the original text, which is somewhat confusing as it is also made out to be a pregnant male entity which is obviously erroneous as only females gets pregnant in reality.

'SECRETS OF ENOCH CHAPTER 26

1 AND I summoned the very lowest a second time, and said: 'Let Archas come forth hard,' and he came forth hard from the invisible.

2 And Archas came forth, hard, heavy, and very red.

3 And I said: 'Be opened, Archas, and let there be born from thee,' and he came undone, an age came forth, very great and very dark, bearing the creation of all lower things, and I saw that *it was* good and said to him:

4 'Go thou down below, and make thyself firm, and be for a foundation for the lower things,' and it happened and he went down and fixed himself, and became the foundation for the lower things, and below the darkness there is nothing else.

C.4 Solomon also talked about the danger of the whorish woman and also equated foolishness as part of the great danger concerning this great whorish entity.

This goddess of Unrighteousness seems to have a lot to do with the spirit of lust. Lust itself seems to be both male and female and thus demonic. In the extreme demonic form known as incubus and succubus.

Proverbs gives all kinds of warnings to young men, in particular, to watch out for the whorish woman who can reduce a man to a piece of bread. In other words, take all of his money and substance. It mentions the dangers of drinking houses and drunkenness as being very dangerous along with Lust.

C.5 The above Book of 2nd Book of Enoch seems to allude to the entity of Adoil as being feminine and giving birth to countless positive Creations. Alternatively, it states that another female entity Archas gave birth to all of the things of Darkness or what was created in the Darkness. The Entity of Light or better known as Wisdom gave birth to another Entity of Light which would appear to be the Son of God.

The verse states that God the Father made Him (the Light entity that had just been born) in charge of all the higher realms of Heaven of the spirit world. The Dark Entity gave birth to all the things of Darkness in the lower realms.

Do we have evidence of this? There are many goddesses throughout history described as both very evil and also powerful and destructive. I think that we would all agree that all of these destructive goddesses came under the jurisdiction of Satan, as I can't find any female entity in books of knowledge and Wisdom that show a female entity of Darkness in a lower position than Satan.

To my way of thinking and according to the Bible, Satan is the entity in charge of the Darkness in general.

C.6 I want to show some verses from Proverbs by Solomon about the extreme danger of some of these beings of darkness or better said demons.

Proverbs .1.8 "My son, hear the instruction of thy father, and forsake not the law of thy mother:"

C.7 This is an interesting verse as it shows both a Father and a Mother. Is this verse only speaking physically? Or is it also referring to God the Father and God the Mother?

Proverbs .1.28 How long, ye simple ones, will ye love simplicity? and the scorners delight in their scorning, and fools hate knowledge?

Proverbs 1.32 For the turning away of the simple shall slay them, And the prosperity of fools shall destroy them

C.8 Watch out about the Strange Woman as mentioned by Solomon. Is this female that Solomon mentions human or demonic or both? It would appear to be the demonic spirit of Lust:

Here is **Proverbs 2.16-19**

[16] To deliver thee from the strange woman, even from the stranger which flatters with her words;

[17] Which forsakes the guide of her youth, and forgets the covenant of her God.

[18] For her house inclines unto death, and her paths unto the dead.

[19] None that go unto her return again, neither take they hold of the paths of life.

C.9 Fitting some of the verses of 2nd Enoch with 1st Enoch chapter 42

Wisdom found no place where she might dwell;
Then a dwelling-place was assigned her in the heavens.
Wisdom went forth to make her dwelling among the children of men,
And found no dwelling-place:
Wisdom/Holy Spirit/ returned to her place,
And took her seat among the angels.
And unrighteousness (Lust) went forth from her chambers:
Whom she sought not she found,
And dwelt with them

C.10 In other words unrighteousness (Lust) found lots of customers down on the earth along with many foolish/unwise people.

PROVERBS CHAPTER 3.5-9

'Get wisdom, get understanding: forget *it* not; neither decline from the words of my mouth. Forsake her not, and she shall preserve thee: love her, and she shall keep thee. Wisdom is the principal thing. Therefore, get Wisdom and with all thy getting get understanding. Exalt her, and she shall promote thee: she shall bring thee to honour, when thou dost embrace her. She shall give to thine head an ornament of grace: a crown of glory shall she deliver to thee.'

The following are quotes from my book: 'Secrets of Enoch Insights' which came out in July 2024:

C.11 'turn not from God before the face of the vain, who made not Heaven and earth, for these shall perish and those who worship them' - Who is Enoch talking about here? He is talking about those who are vain. Vain - definition: without meaning, shallow - or that anything goes.

C.12 Vanity of Vanity for all is vanity

Ecclesiastes 1.2 'Vanity of vanities, saith the Preacher, vanity of vanities; all is vanity- Solomon.:

C.13 Those who rule this present world, and I mean the demonic forces behind the physical rulers - believe that there are no Absolutes, no God, no Jesus, no love, no meaning to life, and therefore there is no consequence to ones actions, so just do anything that you want to do, which is in itself idol worship of devils and demons, because that is exactly what they do and how they behave. They distract most people by getting them to lust after and to eventually worship Mammon or money and riches and popularity and fame come next. They get mankind to constantly strive for vain things which cannot satisfy and then get them addicted to money and things and pleasures which have no lasting value or eternal value.

C.14 The 'vain' entities know that 'The Judgment' is coming, in spite of them pretending to be blind to reality, but they try to forget about it as brought out with the demons talking to Jesus:

Matthew 8.29 Behold, they cried out, saying, 'What have we to do with thee, Jesus, thou Son of God? 'Art thou come hither to torment us before the time?'

INSANITY IN THE WORLD IN 2024 - The Olympic Games. Descent into total madness!

C.15 We saw the insanity of the opening ceremony of the Olympic Games which was totally disgusting and full of satanism. Then we saw a woman boxer get pulverized in just a few punches in the very 1st round of an Olympic boxing match. It turns out the reason was because her opposer was a man dressed up as a woman and a guy that had been banned the year before for not passing the sex test as a woman.

The satanists are trying to destroy God's Creation and to destroy all the godly rules that still exist in today's decadent world. This world is now just like Sodom and Gomorrah of the Old Testament times.

Recently, in the UK it was declared by the British medical council that the word 'mother' would not be used anymore. Now they say men can also be mothers. It sounds like Newspeak from the novel 1984. The idea being to change all the words and their meaning so that the masses get confused and that eventually no one can communicate with each other anymore. Common sense is fast disappearing from our planet. We all saw the madness and severe restrictions placed upon all the populations of the world during the Covid years. We have seen how that millions have died as a direct result of that madness. We now have the insanity of unjustified wars in both Ukraine and the Middle East. There is also an insane problem in the housing market here in the UK and I have been told by others that it is also very difficult in other parts of the world such as the USA, Denmark, New Zealand etc. Christianity is getting bashed in the West as well as other ungodly parts of the world. It is time for men and women of scruples, honour and dignity and faith to stand up for godly morals and values. It saddens me greatly to see the world descending into great darkness!

Obviously, something awful is going to happen! Will it be a sudden nuclear war which destroys the planet? Or will the climate implode as globalists are telling us? What is important is for us to hold on to our faith in God's Word. Only God Himself can save us from the total destruction that is planned by the satanists or globalists. Make sure, that you have a Bible and that you read it on a regular basis.

CHAPTER 6: WHAT IS THE HOLY SPIRIT HERSELF LIKE?

C.1 How do I personally experience Her? She takes away our sorrows and embraces us like a mother with a small child. She fills us with love and anointing to go and tell others about her Son Jesus and about Salvation.

She also encourages us to live like her Son Jesus the Saviour, so that others can get saved too. She teaches us in ways of kindness and caring for others.

C.2 What is the difference in our relationship with her and with Jesus her Son? Jesus is the Word of God. Therefore, we become full of Jesus when we read the Bible as it says so clearly in John.

John 1.1 'In the beginning was the Word and the Word was with God and the same was in the beginning with God. All things were made by Him and without Him was nothing made that was made.

IS THERE A DIFFERENCE IN THE ROLE OF GOD THE FATHER & GOD THE MOTHER?

C.3 In the old days often the father was the disciplinarian, and the mother would comfort the child after the father had spanked the child for his errors or his evil ways. Is that the way it is supposed to be?

As adults, it is a little more complicated. Paul spoke about these things in the New Testament. We are chastened by God for our sins and rightly so. To me the Holy Spirt however is much more like a Comforter, which is also clearly mentioned in the New Testament. She also empowers with wisdom and discernment.

C.4 In the time of Jesus, the Holy Spirit was known as a feminine being or the wife of God the Father.

Here is the translation of the original language that the following verse of **John 14.26** as it was written in Hebrew:-

John 14.26 The Comforter which is the Holy Ghost whom the Father will send in my name, **she** shall teach you all things and bring all things to your remembrance whatsoever I have said unto you.

THERE HAS TO BE A FEMALE IN THE GODHEAD

C.5 It is a law of nature that you don't get children without the woman or the female.

Why is the Trinity shown as 3 masculine Gods when even that does not make any sense at all. You cannot get fruit in nature from only one sex. It takes both masculine and feminine so why not the spirit world also? If it was God in the spirit world who created the physical world, then the physical should be a reflection of the spiritual world in every sense of Creation. Here is some evidence about the Holy Spirit being feminine from my book.

C.6 - SECRETS OF ENOCH INSIGHTS:

Chapter 23.2 2

And Pravuil told me: 'All the things that I have told thee, we have written. Sit and write all the souls of mankind, however many of them are born, and the places prepared for them to eternity; for all souls are prepared to eternity, before the formation of the world.'

John 15.27 "And ye also shall bear witness, because ye have been with me from the beginning."

C.7 Others seem to think that Pravuil was an angel greater in wisdom than all the other archangels, but if that is true, why is Michael known as the chief of the archangels and also the leader of the hosts of heaven. There cannot be an archangel above Michael, so who is Pravuil?

C.8 It would seem that Pravuil is a power above Michael the archangel and the only candidate that would fit the bill is Wisdom herself or the Holy Spirit Mother. There has been a big cover-up by the Catholic church of any beings that are feminine.

C.9 'They' covered up the facts about the Holy Spirit being female and Mother of God. They also covered up the fact that if there are male angels who could have mated with the human women, then there must also be female angels by deduction.

C.10 The Books of Enoch were banned at the council of Laodicea in 364 AD along with all books which stated that the Holy Spirit is female and Mother God.

C.11 Pravuil is like an archangel as mentioned in the Second Book of Enoch who is *quicker in wisdom* than the other archangels and writes all the deeds of the Lord. In the book, God commands Pravuil to get books and a reed of (for) quick writing for Enoch. Pravuil then tells Enoch to "write all the souls of mankind, however many of them are born, and the places prepared for them to eternity". Some scholars have *associated Pravuil with the Holy Spirit.*

C.12 The Catholic church also banned the Books of Enoch for 1000 years on the penalty of being burned at the stake. Why? What were they afraid of? It would seem that the female side of things physical and spiritual has been deliberately erased in the religious and intellectual circles of history.

C.13 Scholars in modern times are becoming aware that the truth has been hidden concerning the Holy Spirit being female. Marianne Widmalm and her book 'Our Mother The Holy Spirit' which came out in 2019 in the USA. Another scholar Ally Kateusz and her book 'Finding Holy Spirit Mother'. These are both excellent books and reveal a lot about the past and how the truth about these matters was deliberately hidden. *The Holy Spirit* is also known as *Wisdom* or *Sophia* in ancient Greek.

C.14 Enoch chapter 42.1 'Wisdom found no place where she might dwell, then a dwelling place was assigned **her** in the heavens.' This was God stressing how on the earth there was a serious lack of wisdom in Pre-Flood times.

C.15 THE TRUTH HAS BEEN HIDDEN

Another very important question to ask oneself is: Has information been hidden from us in the history of the world by the historians and governments of this world? The answer is simple, as the famous British historian Toynbee stated 'The ones who write history are the so-called victors' – the point being that the victors often change the story of what had happened in the past – so that there is a lot of material that is not 100% accurate.

C.16 MOTHER GOD -THE FEMALE HOLY SPIRIT- DIVINE FEMININE

MAT.12:31 Wherefore I say unto you, 'All manner of sin and blasphemy shall be forgiven unto men: but the blasphemy against the Holy Ghost shall not be forgiven unto men.'

MAR.3:29-30 But he that shall blaspheme against the Holy Ghost hath never forgiveness but is in danger of eternal damnation; because they said, He hath an unclean spirit.

LUK.12:10 And whosoever shall speak a word against the Son of man, it shall be forgiven him: but unto him that blasphemes against the Holy Ghost it shall not be forgiven.

C.17 Why did Jesus make a distinction between Himself and the Holy Spirit here? If God and Jesus and the Holy Spirit were all masculine, which is how they are portrayed by most modern churches, then perhaps Jesus would not have made this distinction!

C.18 Let me put in simple terms to understand. A man who has a beautiful wife, whom he both loves and adores, and also has a strong son. If perchance another man comes and gives a blow to his son, it is conceivable that the father will make light of it and forgive the man. However, if the man hits his wife, I guarantee that he would neither forgive him or let him go unpunished. I do think that these above Bible verses prove one thing: The Holy Spirit has got to both feminine and God's wife. Nothing but wrath to those who would hurt and offend her!

Proverbs 3:15-19 "She is more precious than rubies: and all the things thou canst desire are not to be compared unto her. Length of days is in her right hand and in her left-hand riches and honour. Her ways are ways of pleasantness, and all her paths are peace. *She* is a tree of life to them that lay hold upon her: and happy is everyone that retains her. The LORD by wisdom hath founded the earth; by understanding hath he established the heavens."

C.19 Since it is written that God created man in His image, male and female, one might ask is there a possibility the Holy Ghost, the third person of the Trinity is Wisdom. Below are more verses on Wisdom.

Proverbs 1:20-21 Wisdom cries without; she utters her voice in the streets: She cries in the chief place of concourse, in the openings of the gates: in the city she utters her words. So that thou incline thine ear unto wisdom, and apply thine heart to understanding; Yea, if thou cry after knowledge, and lift up thy voice for understanding; If thou seek her as silver, and search for her as for hid treasures,

Proverbs 2:2-4 Get wisdom, get understanding: forget it not; neither decline from the words of my mouth. Forsake her not, and she shall preserve thee: love her, and she shall keep thee. Wisdom is the principal thing; therefore, get wisdom: and with all thy getting get understanding. Exalt her, and she shall promote thee: she shall bring thee to honour, when thou dost embrace her. She shall give to thine head an ornament of grace: a crown of glory shall she deliver to thee.

Proverbs 4:5-9 Say unto wisdom, 'Thou art my sister; and call understanding thy kinswoman':

Proverbs 7:4 Doth not wisdom cry? and understanding put forth her voice? She stands in the top of high places, by the way in the places of the paths. She cries at the gates, at the entry of the city, at the coming in at the doors.

Proverbs 8:1-3 Before the mountains were settled, before the hills was I brought forth: While as yet he had not made the earth, nor the fields, nor the highest part of the dust of the world. When he prepared the heavens, I was there: when he set a compass upon the face of the depth: When he established the clouds above: when he strengthened the fountains of the deep: When he gave to the sea his decree, that the waters should not pass his commandment: when he appointed the foundations of the earth: Then I was by him, as one brought up with him: and I was daily his delight, rejoicing always before him.

Proverbs 8:25-30 Wisdom hath built her house, she hath hewn out her seven pillars: She hath killed her beasts; she hath mingled her wine; she hath also furnished her table. She hath sent forth her maidens: she cries upon the highest places of the city.

C.20 You can know more about the feminine Holy Spirit Mother by reading my recent book 'Secrets of Enoch Insights'.

Chapter 1 It is stated in the 2nd Book of Enoch *'conceived love for him'* This sounds like a *feminine* expression for love. Why does it state it is this way? What if we have God the Father and God the Holy Spirit Mother and God the Son. Then the above expression would make a lot more sense. There are many people today who believe that the Holy Spirit is female.

C.21 Let's imagine for a moment that the ancient Hebrew writings were correct and that the New Testament Jewish Christians were correct - who all stated that the Holy Spirit is female. Jewish law stated in the Old Testament that the 'testimony of two men was true'.

John 8:17: It is also written in your law, that the testimony of two men is true.

C.22 Women can rejoice in the fact that they have a wonderful and fully compassionate Mother in the spirit world -The Holy Spirit, and she is God the Mother, the Father's wife. Jesus is their Son.

I suppose a good question would be why is Jesus the only begotten Son of God the Father and the Holy Spirit Mother and who is Himself also God or Almighty? A fascinating topic indeed!

C.23 Why are there only 3 in the Trinity of the religions and not 4 or more Gods? That is also a very interesting question. God simply states in the Bible that before Him there was no other God. Why is there not a Daughter of God but only the Son of God? The answer to that question is found in the Bride of Christ.

Isaiah 45.5 "I am the Lord, and there is no other; Besides Me there is no God. I will gird you, though you have not known Me;

Exodus 20.3 "You shall have no other gods before Me

C.24 When God states 'I am the Lord and there is no other' He is also talking on behalf of the entire trinity of God: God the Father, the Holy Spirit Mother and Jesus the only begotten Son of God and the Creator.

1 John 5.7 For there are *three* that bear record in heaven, the Father, the Word (Jesus), and the Holy Ghost (Mother): and these three are one.

C.25 From my book 'Secrets of Enoch Insights' (published July 2024): 'In the Slavic version of 2nd Enoch this chapter shows something very interesting as it mentions a being that would appear to be pregnant - Adoil ?

As far as I know only woman or the feminine side of nature can get pregnant. I am not saying that I know the whole picture, but it appears to me that the physical world is a reflection of the much vaster spiritual world.' In our physical world we distinctly see male and female in all of Creation, but these are earthly values are they not? That is what is taught. What if male and female are actually spiritual and eternal values and that they never change. What if this Slavic translation version of The Book of Enoch is doing a clumsy job of trying to state the following:

C.26 In Pre-Creation times there was Almighty God the Father and He was married to a Feminine Goddess of God the Mother. He loved her very much and as women do, she got pregnant. I know this is just a simple illustration as God and the Holy Spirit are infinite and who am I to try and describe them, but I am trying to the best of my ability to make it easier for others to understand, instead of having the concepts of God the Father and the Holy Spirit and God the Son having been made too complicated by the religious institutions - which shy away from many realities of the spirit world.

C.27 Many religious people 'spiritually speaking' seem to me like a person who walks on the beach and gets his toes wet in the seawater, but who never ventures out into the ocean, which is just full of adventure and amazing discoveries. Tradition tells them to stay on the beach and not dive into the waters. Why? Because religious people in general don't ask the right questions of Jesus, God and His Holy Spirit. They tend not to have a personal link with God, where they can ask questions and get answers from God. No, the religious person is too much in a box of traditions to venture out into new possibilities. If anyone suggest something different might be the truth - he is immediately shouted down as being a blasphemer or worse. Just because the majority of religious people believe one thing is right, does not make it right. What does God Himself say about these things? 'Prove Me saith the Lord God'. God likes us to challenge Him as to why things are the way they are.

Malachi 3:10 : Bring ye all the tithes into the storehouse, that there may be meat in mine house, and prove me now herewith, saith the LORD of hosts, if I will not open you the windows of heaven, and pour you out a blessing, that there shall not be room enough to receive it.

C.28 THE 2ND BOOK OF ENOCH CLEARLY SHOWS A FEMININE 'PREGNANT' BEING IN THE GODHEAD

In working on the Book of 2nd Enoch and researching what has been said by theologians and writers it becomes evident that many writers are far too complicated for the average reader to understand. Many so-called experts or professional writers of the past are simply making things far too complicated.

For example, others have not noticed the simple fact that there is a feminine reference to the Godhead in Chapter 25 of 2nd Enoch as it mentions that 'he' has a big belly and later a writer mentions the entity sounds pregnant. Even a small child used to be able to tell you that it is the feminine being that gets pregnant and has babies. I don't know what on earth they are teaching the little children today to the point that there is no longer any male or female and that men can have babies!?. What utter madness. Satan and his ilk are always trying to corrupt the truth and say that 'it ain't necessarily so' to suit an agenda whether it is history or science or organized religions or finance. I think that the problem is that the basics of Creation have not been properly established due to bias in Judeo/Christian beliefs which give the impression that God the Father and God the Holy Spirit and God the Son are all masculine.

C.29 Many religionists obviously don't like the idea that there is a female member of the Trinity in the Holy Spirit Mother.

That should be natural to understand and believe as the rest of God's amazing Creation. All of Creation is male and female and for a very good reason. Satan and the modernists are trying to teach modern man that you don't have to be male or female and that having children is not important.

C.30 God's very first command to the very first man and woman was to procreate and fill the earth with people.

C.31 Today the powers that be are trying to get rid of the populations of the earth through nasty eugenics programs.

Man has departed from the simplicity of Christ and the simplicity that existed in the beginning of Creation before the son of Satan known as Cain came along and committed the very first murder. According to the Jewish Historian, Josephus in circa 100 AD, Cain was the first to use weights and measures. Cain was in fact the very first deceptive merchant. Josephus goes on to state that Cain increased his substance by lying and cheating and teaching mankind to stray away from the original simplicity that God had taught them.

Education has often educated man out of faith and into disbelief. To have faith in God one has to believe the Word of God and not put up with the adulterated truths. There are certain basics to believe in if one is to believe in and follow the Bible for our education. It is very important to stick with what the apostle Paul stated in the New Testament.

2 Corinthians 11.3 'I fear least by any means as the Serpent beguiled Eve through his subtlety that your minds should be corrupted from the simplicity that is in Christ.

C.32 From my book Secrets of Enoch Insights which is based on the 2nd Book of Enoch: '

What was going on in the Pre-Creation times before God had created the spirit world or the physical world or all the beings of heaven and earth?' Well, some scholars or writers try to make this chapter too intangible or ethereal or imaginary for my liking, when it seems plain that the story of Adoil and Archas in the 2nd Book of Enoch, , it is not just talking about an age of time (intangible) but talking about entities that have the direct authority from God to be in charge of things. God has made one entity in charge of the Light and higher dimensions and another in charge of all the lower dimensions or the Darkness. These entities appear to be female by virtue of the fact that it states that they were pregnant. Male beings do not get pregnant, that we know for certain. That is what chapters 25-26 appear to be saying.

C.33 GOD'S LOVE FOR THE HOLY SPIRIT MOTHER

Spiritually speaking in simple physical language, God is love according to the Bible, I think that in eternity God the Father and God the Holy Spirit loved each other very much and the result was that the Holy Spirit got pregnant. Not necessarily in the physical way we think, but as someone has wisely mentioned when a man and woman are together, and they love each other. Then often the woman gets pregnant. The man or husband is thinking of a few things like the woman and perhaps how to take care of her. The woman however is thinking of 20 other relevant things such as where are they going to live, if children come along, and how will they best take care of themselves and what will they dress them in, and where to go and buy the clothes for the children; and where will they go to school etc?

Since God is an eternal being and likewise so is also the Holy Spirit, what if in Eternity, God the Father and God the Holy Spirit Mother went through stages of love such as we humans, who are reflections of God go through?

Such as love when we are young or even teenagers and then when love gets a bit more serious, and the women is ready for pregnancy. This is the most important time for the woman. She needs her man's protection more than ever before, and His supply and his assurance and comfort. She is happy to be pregnant, but she needs constant reassurance.

2nd Enoch seems to state that a time came when the Holy Spirit was pregnant with millions of creations that as yet had not been made manifest, and so God the Father stated 'Let's make a dimension where all of your creations can become a reality and thus both the Spirit world first of all, and as a reflection the physical world was also created.

C.34 The Bible states that Jesus was the beginning of the Creation of God. Then God the Father and the Trinity created the angels and spiritual beings and heaven itself. Once that was all established eventually, they created the physical dimensions.

All the feminine creations were also manifest in these creations, so as to make the Creation itself very colourful and well-balanced.

C.35 Creation could not have been made by an all male Godhead. That does not make any sense.

It is the woman's touches that make all the difference in a home.

VERSE 5 And I placed for myself a throne, and took my seat on it, and said to the light: 'Go thou up higher and fix thyself high above the throne and be a foundation to the highest things.' God the Father talking to his Son Jesus, telling him to be in charge of the light and all the higher dimensions. This all happened before the Creation of the physical dimensions. Jesus stated that He was the 'light of the world' in John chapter 8.

C.36 I am convinced that it was Jesus who was the creator of the physical world, but that He had a lot of help from His Mother the Holy Spirit in creating things to get the right colours and to make the male/female balance as stated so well in Genesis 'Let us create man in our image and male and female created He them.' Who was God talking to unless it was a female – the Holy Spirit Mother?

Genesis 1.26-27 And God said, let us make man in our image, after our likeness: and let them have dominion over the fish of the sea, and over the fowl of the air, and over the cattle, and over all the earth, and over every creeping thing that creepeth upon the earth. So God created man in his own image, in the image of God created he him; <u>male and female</u> created he them.

C.37 I think this explanation has some merit. We all know that the Gospel of John states that in the beginning was the Word and the Word was with God and the Word was God. Jesus was the Creator of this physical universe as He is also known as the Son of God. If the Holy Spirit is thus His divine Mother then it would have been Jesus with the help of His Holy Spirit Mother and Father doing the original creation of the physical world. It would appear that it was God the Father and the Holy Spirit Mother that created the spiritual world. The Bible teaches that Jesus was the beginning of the Creation of God.

Revelation 3.14 "And unto the angel of the church of the Laodiceans write; These things saith the Amen, the faithful and true witness, the <u>beginning of the creation of God</u>;"

C.38 With the concept of the Holy Spirit being the perfect Mother everything makes much more sense in looking at the Creation itself. It states in Genesis that God created us in His image and then succinctly states and male and female created He them. Who was God talking to if not the female Holy Spirit His eternal companion. Thinking like this brings a whole new reality to love and romance and love itself. Everyone needs to taste of love itself, and it is my hope and prayer that eventually everyone who is godly will find the perfect soulmate.

C.39 If Jesus was the one who created the physical dimension, one thing for sure is that He had lots of help not just from God the Father but from God the Mother who put her beautiful myriad of touches to Creation with all of its thousands of variety of flowers and trees and creatures with all of their amazing colours. Macho religions have pushed our precious Holy Spirit Mother completely out of the picture which simply does not work. Love is everything in this universe in its many forms. Without the female side of things there is no future! It is as simple as that.

Isaiah 65.18 But be ye glad and rejoice for ever in that which I create: for, behold, I create Jerusalem a rejoicing, and her people a joy.

C.40 There are so many very interesting details in the 2nd Book of Enoch that are just fascinating. None more so than the Pre-Creation Story. It is sad that many of the religionists and the scholars of religion are so tied up in ancient dogma of 'male chauvinist religion dominance' that they can't even work it out that only women give birth to babies and that Creation itself has a Mother in the form of the Holy Spirit Mother as mentioned in 2nd Enoch chapter 25, which is not very difficult to prove.

CHAPTER 7: THE WOMB

Revelation 12:1-3 "And there appeared a great wonder in heaven; a woman clothed with the sun, and the moon under her feet, and upon her head a crown of twelve stars: And she being with child cried, travailing in birth, and pained to be delivered. And she brought forth a man child, who was to rule all nations with a rod of iron: and her child was caught up unto God, and to his throne."

C.1 Here we see a pregnant woman in heaven about to give birth to a man child who is to "rule all nations with a rod of iron" She with the crown of 12 stars is supposed to represent the true church of Christ. We know this prophecy has not been fulfilled and will not be fulfilled until the second coming of Jesus. He certainly did not rule all nations with a rod of iron upon His first coming.

Psalm 2 speaks of this same event:

Psalm 2:9 "Thou shalt break them with a rod of iron; thou shalt dash them in pieces like a potter's vessel."

Here is another case where pregnancy is mentioned:

Luke 1:30-35 "And the angel said unto her, Fear not, Mary: for thou hast found favour with God. And, behold, thou shalt conceive in thy womb, and bring forth a son, and shalt call his name Jesus. He shall be great and shall be called the Son of the Highest: and the Lord God shall give unto him the throne of his father David: And he shall reign over the house of Jacob for ever; and of his kingdom there shall be no end. Then said Mary unto the angel, How shall this be, seeing I know not a man? And the angel answered and said unto her, The Holy Ghost shall come upon thee, and the power of the Highest shall overshadow thee: therefore, also that holy thing which shall be born of thee shall be called the Son of God."

C.2 Continuing in Luke 1, one of the first things Mary does after receiving this message from Gabriel is to visit her cousin Elisabeth who is six months pregnant with John the Baptist. As soon as Elisabeth hears Mary's greeting the babe leaped in her womb.

Luke 1 "And it came to pass, that, when Elisabeth heard the salutation of Mary, the babe leaped in her womb; and Elisabeth was filled with the Holy Ghost."

C.3 Obviously the *"womb"* is of tremendous importance both spiritually and physically. However, only females or women can get pregnant. Certainly not men and that was God's original intent. There is only 'Male and Female', as Trump announced at his Inauguration on the 20th January 2025.

C.4 Three other verses in which "womb" could almost be interpreted as somewhat of an enigma are:

Psalm 110:3 "Thy people shall be willing in the day of thy power, in the beauties of holiness from the womb of the morning."

Job 38:8,29 "And I shut up the sea with gates, when it rushed out, coming forth out its mother's womb." "Out of whose womb comes the ice?"

Genesis 25:23 "And the Lord said to her, there are two nations in thy womb."

C.5 Here we have the Lord speaking of the sea coming out of its mother's womb, ice coming out of a womb and two nations coming from Rebecca's's womb. Very mysterious occurrences. When you think about two nations coming from the womb of a woman it sounds, well, unusual.

C.6 Obviously, pregnancy, the womb, and deliverance both spiritually and physically are fundamentally essential for our redemption.

Ecclesiasticus 1.16 The fear of the Lord Is the beginning of wisdom, and was created with the faithful in the womb, it walketh with chosen women, and is known with the just and faithful.

PROVERBS 8 "Thou shalt proclaim wisdom, that understanding may be obedient to thee. For she is on lofty eminences and stands in the midst of the ways. For she sits by the gates of princes and sings in the entrances. The Lord made me in the beginning of his ways for his works. He established me before time was in the beginning, before he made the earth: even before he made the depths; before the fountains of water came forth: before the mountains were settled, and before all hills, he begat me. The Lord made countries and uninhabited tracks, and the highest inhabited parts of the world. When he prepared the heaven, I was present with him; and when he prepared his throne upon the winds: and when he strengthened the clouds above; and when he secured the fountains of the earth: and when he strengthened the foundations of the earth: I was by him, *suiting* myself to him, I was that wherein he took delight; and daily I rejoiced in his presence continually."

C.7 Wisdom, as is very clear, is referred to in the feminine pronoun.

'I was by him, *suiting* myself to him, I was that wherein he took delight; and daily I rejoiced in his presence continually."

C.8 This verse certainly sounds like a couple courting or very much in love with each other.

C.9 Incidentally the *Shekinah Glory*, which rested between the wings of the Cherubim on the mercy seat atop the Ark of the Covenant, was a feminine representation of the glory of God. Could the Shekinah Glory have been the Holy Spirit Mother?

Genesis 1:6-8 "And God said, Let there be a firmament in the midst of the water, and let it be a division between water and water, and it was so. And God made the firmament, and God divided between the water which was under the firmament and the water which was above the firmament. And God called the firmament Heaven, and God saw that it was good, and there was evening and there was morning, the second day."

Genesis 7:11 "In the six hundredth year of the life of Noe, in the second month, on the twenty-seventh day of the month, on this day all the fountains of the abyss were broken up, and the floodgates (windows) of heaven were opened."

Job 38:8,29 "And I shut up the sea with gates, when it rushed out, coming forth out its mother's womb." "Out of whose womb comes the ice?"

C.10 In studying this verse it appears to be talking about the Northern entrance or (where the North Pole is supposed to be). There are in fact holes at the poles which descend inside a hollow earth with seas on the underside of the earth. In the Northern opening there is an ice barrier of several hundred feet high in the area where one cannot see either the outer sun or the inner sun. There are many scientific reports about these facts. Including the explorer Admiral Byrd of the USA back in 1926 and 1947.

C.11 Is the Earth in Fact Hollow? (See my website: www.insightspublication.com)

The apocryphal book of 2nd Esdras which was in the KJV of the Bible until the 19th century. God mentions in this amazing book that the earth is hollow. This book was written by the prophet Ezra circa 500 BC. Here are some verses from that book which you will also find in my book 'Esdras Insights', which came out August 2023.

2ND ESDRAS CH 4.23 And I said," No lord, it cannot". And he said to me, "In Hades the chambers of the souls are like the *womb*" "For just as a woman who is in travail makes haste to escape the pangs of birth, so also do these places hasten to give back those things that were committed to them from the beginning; then the things that you desire to see will be disclosed to you.

C.12 Here is stated that nothing is random in God's Creation but that all is done in order and at the right time.

2ND ESDRAS CH 5.30 He said to me 'Even so have I given the *womb of the earth* to those who from time to time are *sown in it*, for as an infant does not bring forth, and a woman who has become old does not bring forth and longer, so have I organized the world that I have created.

C.13 THE APOCRYPHON OF JOHN which was written before 185 AD states the following about the Holy Spirit – 'And His (God the Father) thought performed a deed and she came forth, namely she who had appeared before him in the shine of His light.'

This is the first power which was before all of them and which came forth from his mind, She is the forethought of the All - her light shines like His light -the perfect power which is the image of the invisible, virginal Spirit who is perfect.

FALSE PIETY

C.14 Why do the religions like to use this word virginal? It is almost as if it is supposed to be a sacred word. However, its use is often totally misplaced. How can the women mentioned both be mothers and virginal. Someone somewhere does not understand the basics of sex. Both Mary the mother of Jesus and the Holy Spirit Mother are mothers. OK, in the case of Mary of Joseph she was virginal before Jesus was born but certainly did not stay that way, as Jesus had many brothers and sisters who were born to His physical mother Mary.

C.15 This inevitably reminds us of the Wisdom texts in Proverbs, which describe her as God's first Creation or emanation, and a reflection, or radiance, of His light and an image of His goodness. It goes on to say 'she became the *womb* of everything for it is she who is prior to them all.

C.16 Christ is described as the Word and the Light following the Gospel of John. The Holy Spirit is the Mother of all living. Sophia which is the Greek word for Wisdom is called 'Life which is the Mother of all living'.

C.17 The Holy Spirit is also known as Wisdom in the Hebrew Old Testament and also known as the character Adoil in chapter 25 of '2nd Enoch' or my book 'Secrets of Enoch Insights'. Adoil, was supposedly the mother of all the good things throughout time.

C.18 The Holy Spirit is Mother God and the mother of Jesus. In fact She is Mother and Creator of all the female side of the Creation. She is Wisdom as mentioned clearly in Proverbs 8 and many other Proverbs as well as other passages in the KJV Bible.

Author: I admit that this is my theory about the Feminine Holy Spirit being largely responsible for the creation of the feminine side of God's Creation.

C.19 There was God the Father and God the Mother according to 25th chapter of 2nd Enoch and then was a supernatural birth and then born the Son of God Jesus who was made in charge of all the higher realms or dimensions of light.

CHAPTER 8: ECCLESIASTICUS - WISDOM OF BEN SIRIACH

Comment.1 Look at the following amazing verses about the Holy Spirit Mother from

ECCLESIASTICUS - Chapter 24.

24.1 Wisdom shall praise herself and shall glory in the midst of her people.

C.2 Wisdom shall praise herself. I believe that it should state 'Wisdom is Praise'.

IS THE HOLY SPIRIT THE SPIRIT OF PRAISE

I believe that it should state '**Wisdom *is* praise**'

When I think about heaven and the throne of God I think of God's throne and God is surrounded by angels and Cherubim and Seraphim and great multitudes of peoples and what are they invariably doing? They are all praising God. Why are they praising God and what is the purpose of praising? I think that we all know the answers to these questions. Praise is acknowledging that God is the boss and that we are thankful for all that He does for us. Praise also shows that we love God and want to be in His presence. Let's face it: God is worthy of being praised as He has done so much for all of us. I can't think of anybody else who deserves our praise and worship as He has created all things for our joy and pleasure. I would say that one of the strong points that I have seen is when I see people praising the Lord and singing. *Is it just possible that the Holy Spirit Herself is the one who encourages everyone to both praise and worship God.* As She is a Mother She directs all of us her children to learn to praise God so that *we can get close to Him.* It really is not that difficult when we start praising God for His Creation and His supply and blessings and His taking care of everything.

24.9 He created me from the beginning before the world, and I shall never fail.

Proverbs 8.22-23 The Lord possessed me in the beginning of his way, before his works of old.

I was set up from everlasting, from the beginning, or ever the earth was.

24.18 I am the Mother of fair love, and fear (of the Lord) and knowledge and Holy hope: I therefore being eternal, am given to all my children which are named of Him.

Acts 1.8 Ye shall receive power after that the Holy Ghost is come upon you and ye shall be witnesses unto Me.

C.3 This verse **Ecclesiasticus - Chapter 24.18** in particular is showing so much truth. First of all, Wisdom states that she is the one who brings real love to people, as well as the fact that she teaches about the fear of the Lord in such a way that her children can learn and have hope through God. Wisdom/Holy Spirit states that she herself is eternal. In other words she was with God the Father long before the Creation of the physical earth happened. She is the wife of God the Father and their Son is Jesus Christ. The Holy Spirit says that She is given to all of her children which are named of Him. Who is Him – none other than Jesus who is the very 1st begotten of God the Father and God the Mother.

24.19 Come unto me, all ye that be desirous of me, and fill yourselves with my fruits.

C.4 Here is the entire chapter which is amazing.

It is amazing how the Holy Spirit Mother describes herself. She describes herself as Wisdom that we should all desire. Why? Because She will cause us to become fruitful in our mission for Christ.

Proverbs 8.35 Whoso finds Me (Wisdom) finds life and obtains favour of the Lord.

Proverbs 18.22 Whoso finds a wife obtains a good thing and obtains favour of the Lord.

C.5 Look how similar these above two Bible verse are. Why are they so similar? Why does Wisdom compare Herself to being a wife? Because *She* is Love personified.

C.6 Does God the Father or God the Mother get involved in the love and sexual relationships of human beings? That is an obvious question, that they obviously do and they encourage good marriages and the birth of babies and families.

C.7 When Jesus was born of Mary it clearly states in scripture that both God the Father and God the Mother were involved in the conception of baby Jesus.

Luke 1.35 And the angel answered and said unto her, "The Holy Ghost shall come upon thee, and the power of the Highest shall overshadow thee. Therefore, also that Holy Being who shall be born of thee shall be called the Son of God.

C.8 BEN SIRACH Chapter 24

1 Wisdom shall praise herself, and shall glory in the midst of her people.

C.9 I believe that it should state Wisdom is praise.

2 In the congregation of the Most High shall she open her mouth, and triumph before his power.

3 I came out of the mouth of the Most High and covered the earth as a cloud.

4 I dwelt in high places, and my throne is in a cloudy pillar.

5 I alone compassed the circuit of heaven and walked in the bottom of the deep.

6 In the waves of the sea and in all the earth, and in every people and nation, I got a possession.

7 With all these I sought rest: and in whose inheritance shall I abide?

8 So the Creator of all things gave me a commandment, and he that made me caused my tabernacle to rest, and said, Let thy dwelling be in Jacob, and thine inheritance in Israel.

9 He created me from the beginning before the world, and I shall never fail.

10 In the holy tabernacle I served before him; and so was I established in Sion.

11 Likewise in the beloved city he gave me rest, and in Jerusalem was my power.

12 And I took root in an honourable people, even in the portion of the Lord's inheritance.

13 I was exalted like a cedar in Libanus, and as a cypress tree upon the mountains of Hermon.

14 I was exalted like a palm tree in En-gaddi, and as a rose plant in Jericho, as a fair olive tree in a pleasant field, and grew up as a plane tree by the water.

15 I gave a sweet smell like cinnamon and aspalathus, and I yielded a pleasant odour like the best myrrh, as galbanum, and onyx, and sweet storax, and as the fume of frankincense in the tabernacle.

16 As the turpentine tree I stretched out my branches, and my branches are the branches of honour and grace.

17 As the vine brought I forth pleasant savour, and my flowers are the fruit of honour and riches.

18 I am the mother of fair love, and fear, and knowledge, and holy hope: I therefore, being eternal, am given to all my children which are named of him.

19 Come unto me, all ye that be desirous of me, and fill yourselves with my fruits.

20 For my memorial is sweeter than honey, and mine inheritance than the honeycomb.

21 They that eat me shall yet be hungry, and they that drink me shall yet be thirsty.

22 He that obeyeth me shall never be confounded, and they that work by me shall not do amiss.

23 All these things are the book of the covenant of the most high God, even the law which Moses commanded for an heritage unto the congregations of Jacob.

24 Faint not to be strong in the Lord; that he may confirm you, cleave unto him: for the Lord Almighty is God alone, and beside him there is no other Saviour.

25 He filleth all things with his wisdom, as Phison and as Tigris in the time of the new fruits.

26 He maketh the understanding to abound like Euphrates, and as Jordan in the time of the harvest.

27 He maketh the doctrine of knowledge appear as the light, and as Geon in the time of vintage.

28 The first man knew her not perfectly: no more shall the last find her out.

29 For her thoughts are more than the sea, and her counsels profounder than the great deep.

30 I also came out as a brook from a river, and as a conduit into a garden.

31 I said, I will water my best garden, and will water abundantly my garden bed: and, lo, my brook became a river, and my river became a sea.

32 I will yet make a doctrine to shine as the morning and will send forth her light afar off.

33 I will yet pour out doctrine as prophecy, and leave it to all ages for ever.

34 Behold that I have not laboured for myself only, but for all them that seek wisdom.

C.10 It is this intimate relationship that God the Father and God the Mother have with their own children that Satan has been trying to get rid of by bringing in perversions as in the story of Sodom and Gomorrah. I am convinced that is why in 364 AD at the council of Laodicea she the Holy Spirit Mother was banned by the devils in the Catholic church. Devils don't like the feminine side of God's creation, as the devils are all perverts as shown in the Books of Enoch as the spirits of the giants who when they died became the disembodied spirits of the giants who after the Great Flood came back from the negative spirit world according to the Hebrew Book of Jubilees and became the Demons.

C.11 Origin of the Demons: It would appear that the original Giants in Pre-Flood times all became perverts because there were no women giants that were born as offspring to the Fallen angels and the human women.

Why did that happen? That is a whole topic in itself and a very interesting question.

Intimate relationship with God in the spirit world.

C.12 The truth is that those who are genuinely saved by grace will have a much more intimate relationship with God through their Son Jesus Christ who has called all the saved male or female the Bride of Christ. Scripture also tells us that.

Galatians 3.28 'There is no male or female in Christ Jesus'. This simply means that whether you are a man or a women you are both equally entitled to Salvation through Christ Jesus.

Here is Chapter 1 from this amazing book of Ecclesiasticus by Ben Sirach:

C.13: ECCLESIASTICUS- BEN SIRACH CHAPTER 1

1 All *wisdom* is from the Lord God, and hath been always with him, and is before all time.

2 Who hath numbered the sand of the sea, and the drops of rain, and the days of the world? Who hath measured the height of heaven, and the breadth of the earth, and the depth of the abyss?

3 Who hath searched out the wisdom of God that goeth before all things?

4 Wisdom hath been created before all things, and the understanding of prudence from everlasting.

5 The word of God on high is the fountain of wisdom, and *her* ways are everlasting commandments.

6 To whom hath the root of wisdom been revealed, and who hath known *her* wise counsels?

7 To whom hath the discipline of wisdom been revealed and made manifest? and who hath understood the multiplicity of her steps?

8 There is one most high Creator Almighty, and a powerful king, and greatly to be feared, who sits upon his throne, and is the God of dominion.

9 He created her in the Holy Ghost, and saw her, and numbered her, and measured her.

10 And he poured her out upon all his works, and upon all flesh according to his gift, and

14 The love of God is honourable wisdom.

15 And they to whom she shall shew herself love her by the sight, and by the knowledge of her great works.

16 The fear of the Lord Is the beginning of *wisdom,* and was created with the faithful in the *womb*, it walketh with *chosen women,* and is known with the just and faithful.

C.14 This verse clearly links Wisdom with the womb, and she being feminine bringeth forth and gives life to Gods people. Wisdom is the Divine Feminine. She is the same as the Holy Spirit and together they make the Holy Spirit Mother.

20 To fear God is the fulness of *wisdom*, and fulness is from the fruits thereof.

21 She shall fill all her house with her increase, and the storehouses with her treasures.

22 The fear of the Lord is a crown of wisdom, filling up peace and the fruit of salvation:

C.15 Very interesting to see this observation in the Old Testament. In New Testament times according to the Book of Acts first the person got saved and as a follower then received the Holy Spirit of Wisdom to enable him to witness to others about Jesus and Salvation. This verse shows how interconnected Jesus the Messiah and the Holy Spirit are.

Acts 1.8 But ye shall receive power, after that the Holy Ghost is come upon you: and ye shall be witnesses unto me both in Jerusalem, and in all Judaea, and in Samaria, and unto the uttermost part of the earth.

ECCLESIASTICUS- BEN SIRACH CH 1 (continued)

23 And it hath seen, and numbered her: but both are the gifts of God.

24 Wisdom shall distribute knowledge and understanding of prudence: and exalts the glory of them that hold her.

25 The root of wisdom is to fear the Lord: and the branches thereof are long lived.

26 In the treasures of wisdom is understanding, and religiousness of knowledge: but to sinners wisdom is an abomination.

29 A patient man shall bear for a time, and afterwards joy shall be restored to him.

30 A good understanding will hide his words for a time, and the lips of many shall declare his wisdom.

31 In the treasures of wisdom is the signification of discipline:

33 Son, if thou desire wisdom, keep justice, and God will give her to thee.

34 For the fear of the Lord is wisdom and discipline: and that which is agreeable to him,

35 Is faith, and meekness: and he will fill up his treasures.

THE DIVINE FEMININE

C.16 In order to understand the Old Testament, it is best to study in Hebrew or Hebrew directly translated into modern English today as we speak. There have been many alterations to the original Hebrew as in regard to the Holy Spirit Mother and Wisdom which are the very same Mother God. It is tragic to realise how that scriptures have been deliberately adulterated to fit religious macho agenda and deliberately exclude the feminine side of the Godhead. Why have so many translators been so afraid of the feminine side of things? Well, when we study history, we find the answers.

WHY HAS THE DIVINE FEMININE BEEN OBSOLETED?

No 1. It has been men and not women who have started all the wars on our planet. Men have largely subdued women in most cultures since the time of the Great Flood. Why is that? Well, there is a reason. Relevance? Men are much more violent than women and tend to push others around or even out of their way when it suits their purpose and many of the leaders follow the horrific example of the demons when it comes to violence.

No.2 Since the year 364 AD because of the Catholic edict of Laodicea the feminine side of the church was banned and in particular the knowledge of the Holy Spirit being Mother God.

No.3 The good news is that the influence of the Holy Spirit Mother will soon become much greater in the 'not too distant' future. It has been stated that in the Old Testament Times that God the Father was in charge. It is also stated that after the resurrection of Christ, that Christ has been the one ruling in the background of all Creation. It has been also stated that it will be the Holy Spirit Mother who will rule in the background during the coming Millennium. Think of a much gentler world at least for a season –'The Lion shall lie down with the lamb' ….Isaiah Chapter 11.

Isaiah 11.6-9 The wolf also shall dwell with the lamb, and the leopard shall lie down with the kid; and the calf and the young lion and the fatling together; and a little child shall lead them. And the cow and the bear shall feed; their young ones shall lie down together: and the lion shall eat straw like the ox. And the sucking child shall play on the hole of the asp, and the weaned child shall put his hand on the cockatrice' den. They shall not hurt nor destroy in all my holy mountain: for the earth shall be full of the knowledge of the LORD, as the waters cover the sea.

No.4 It is easy to prove that even Jesus and his disciples called the Holy Spirit Mother God. In the Old Testament the Holy Spirit was referred to as Wisdom. There are many apocryphal books which are still in the Catholic and orthodox Bibles to this day, such as *Ecclesiasticus* (Ben Sirach).

Look at the amazing examples from 'Wisdom of Solomon'.

Wisdom of Solomon 7.22-23: 'For Wisdom, the fashioner of all things, taught me. For in her there is a spirit that is intelligent, holy, unique, manifold, subtle, mobile, clear, unpolluted, distinct, invulnerable, loving the good, keen, irresistible, all-powerful, overseeing all. And penetrating through all spirits, that are intelligent and pure and most subtle…

Wisdom of Solomon 7.27 Though she is but one, she can do all things, and while remaining in herself, she renews all things; in every generation she passes into holy souls and makes them friends of God and *prophets*

Wisdom of Solomon 10.16 She entered the soul of a servant of the Lord and withstood dread kings and wonders and signs. Wisdom does not only enter people, but she is the one sent out to answer prayers.

Wisdom of Solomon 7.7-10: Therefore, I prayed and understanding was given me; I called upon God and the spirit of Wisdom come to me. He created her in the Holy Ghost, and saw her, and numbered her, and measured her. And he poured her out upon all his works, and upon all flesh according to his gift, and hath given her to them that love him.

CHAPTER 9: Writers and Books of the New &Old Testaments

C.1 Early Christian writers 1) Origen 2) Clement of Alexandria 3) Cyril of Jerusalem 4) Jerome.

Jerome studied the gospel of the Hebrews and compared it to the gospel of Matthew. He quoted a lost saying from the Gospel of the Hebrews.

C.2 When Jesus was baptised in the river Jorden by his cousin John the Baptist, the Holy Spirit Mother descended like a dove and a heavenly voice spoke:

(Mark 1:11: Luke 3.22: Matthew 3.17): And there came a voice from heaven, saying, 'Thou art my beloved Son, in whom I am well pleased.'

C.3 The following as also written in the Gospel of the Hebrews: 'The Saviour says: Even so did My Mother, the Holy Spirit, take me by one of my hairs and carry me away onto the great mountain Tabor'.

Mount Tabor: Mount Tabor, sometimes spelled Mount Thabor (Arabic جبل روباط; Hebrew: הר תבור or Har Tavor), is a large hill of biblical significance in Lower Galilee, Northern Israel at the eastern end of the Jezreel Valley, 18 kilometres (11 miles) west of the Sea of Galilee. In the Hebrew Bible (Joshua, Judges), Mount Tabor is the site of the Battle of Mount Tabor between the Israelite army under the leadership of Barak and the army of the Canaanite king of Hazor, Jabin, commanded by Sisera. In Christian tradition, Mount Tabor is the site of the transfiguration of Jesus Mount Tabor - Wikipedia

C.4 LIST OF THE BOOKS OF THE OLD TESTAMENT TALKING ABOUT THE SPIRIT OF GOD BEING THE DIVINE FEMININE:

[Editor: **She** is in **bold** to emphasis the **Holy Spirit feminine.**]

1) PROVERBS

8.1 Doth not wisdom cry? And understanding put forth her voice? **She** stands in the top of high places, by the way in the places of the paths. **She** cries at the gates, at the entry of the city, at the coming in at the doors.

2) BEN SIRACH (ECCLESIATICUS)

Ben Sirach is one of the canonized books in the Catholic Bible & Greek and Russian Orthodox Bibles.

[Editor: Sometimes *She* is in *italics* to emphasis the *Holy Spirit feminine.*]

QUOTE: All wisdom comes from the Lord and is with Him forever. The sand of the sea, the drops of the rain, and the days of eternity – who can count them? The height of the heaven, the breadth of the earth the abyss and Wisdom – Who can search them out? Wisdom was created before all things, and prudent understanding from eternity. The root of Wisdom – to whom had it been revealed? *Her* clever devices – who knows them? There is one who is wise greatly to be feared, sitting upon His throne. The Lord Himself created *Wisdom*; He saw *Her* and appointed *Her*, he poured *Her* out and upon all of his works. *She* dwells with all flesh according to his gift and he supplied *Her* to those who love Him.

3) WISDOM OF SOLOMON.

Quote: For *She* is the *breath of the power of God*, and a pure emanation of the Glory of the Almighty; therefore nothing defiled gains entrance into her. For *She* is a reflection of eternal light, a spotless mirror of the working of God, and an image of His goodness.

Look at other examples from Wisdom of Solomon.

Wisdom of Solomon 7.22-23: 'For Wisdom, the fashioner of all things, taught me. For in her there is a spirit that is intelligent, holy, unique, manifold, subtle, mobile, clear, unpolluted, distinct, invulnerable, loving the good, keen, irresistible, all-powerful, overseeing all. And penetrating through all spirts, that are intelligent and pure and most subtle.

Wisdom of Solomon 7.27 Though she is but one, she can do all things, and while remaining in herself, she renews all things; in every generation she passes into holy souls and makes them friends of God and prophets.

Wisdom of Solomon 10.16 She entered the soul of a servant of the Lord and withstood dread kings and wonders and signs. Wisdom does not only enter people, but she is the one sent out to answer prayers.

Wisdom of Solomon 7.7: Therefore, I prayed and understanding was given me; I called upon God and the spirit of Wisdom come to me.

9 He created her in the *Holy Ghost*, and saw her, and *numbered her*, and *measured her*.

C.5 What do these expressions mean: *numbered her and measured her*. This simply means that God the Father tested Her and found Her to be of great value.

10 And he *poured her out upon all his works, and upon all flesh according to his gift, and hath given her to them that love him.*

C.6 List of The Books of the Early Christian Fathers and Apostles and Writers which directly wrote about the Holy Spirit being a feminine goddess.

They All Believed that The Holy Spirit Is Our Mother God in Heaven and part of The Trinity of God the Father, God the Mother and God the Son:

The following books were highly regarded in the early days of Christianity

1) Shepherd of Hermas

2) Epistle of Barnabus

3) The Apocalypse of Peter

4) Didache

5) Silvanus

6) Teachings of Silvanus (1st to 3rd century) found in Nag Hammadi in Coptic and originally in Greek.

QUOTE: 'My child, return to your first Father, God, and Wisdom, your *Mother,* from whom you came into being from the beginning. Return , that you might fight against all of your enemies, the power of the adversary.

7) Acts of Thomas - QUOTE:

Come, Holy Name of Christ, that is above every name.

Come, Power of the Most High and perfect compassion;

Come highest gift;

Come compassionate Mother

Come, fellowship of the male;

Come, you that reveals the hidden mysteries;

Come, mother of the 7 houses, that your rest many be in the 8th house;

Come, elder messenger of the five members – understanding, thought, prudence, consideration, reasoning,

Communicate with these young men!

Come Holy Spirit, and purify their reins and their heart

And give them the added seal in the name of the Father and the Son and Holy Spirit.

C.7 Another very important book was the *Apocryphon of John* (185 AD)

Quote – And a deed and *She* came forth, she who had appeared before Him in the shine of His light. This is the first power which was before all of them which came forth from His mind. *She* is the forethought of the All -her light shines like His light – the perfect power which is the image of the invisible, virginal Spirit who is perfect.

THE APOCRYPHON OF JOHN mentions Christ described as the 'Word of God' and light. The Holy Spirit is also called 'The Mother of the living' and she is also called Sophia which is the Greek word for Wisdom.

QUOTE: 'Life which is the Mother of the living, by the knowledge of the sovereignty of heaven.'

The Holy Spirit and Wisdom are described as the same Deity.' - The Greek word Sophia is also mentioned as Sophia of Epinoia. In the Book of Genesis Eve was created in the likeness of Epinoia. This would mean that Eve was created in the image of a female God wisdom - or the Holy Spirit Mother.

C.8 THE DEAD SEA SCROLLS: The original authors of the Dead Sea Scrolls which were found at Qumran in 1947 were apocalyptic and adhered to Wisdom (Sophia) or Divine Feminine teachings. –

QUOTE 'Blessed are those who seek her with pure hands, and do not pursue her with a treacherous heart. Bless is the man who has attained Wisdom, and walks in the Law of the Most High. He directs his heart towards her ways and restrains himself by her corrections, and always takes delight in her chastisements.'

GOSPEL OF BARTHOLOMEW

Bartholomew called out to the heavenly Mother

O Womb more spacious than a city!

O Womb wider than the span of heaven!

O Womb that contained him whom the seven heavens do not!

GOSPEL OF LUKE: 3.22

C.9 Originally it stated in the earliest copies of the Gospel of Luke that when Jesus was baptised by John the Baptist in the living waters of the river Jordan, the Holy Spirit stated to her Son Jesus *'Today I have given you birth'*. This saying was removed by scribes due to Catholic edicts from Rome.

C.10 The organized church in general does not represent God but Satan and his lies and deceptions as the church worships Mammon idols and not Christ Jesus. The organized churches give lip service to Christ but do not do what he said to do in the 4 gospels which spell out clearly what it means to be a Christian.

C.11 There are found baptismal fonts from the late 300 AD such as the Basilica of St Vitalis, North Africa with a stone womb for the members to get baptised in. At their own baptisms early Christians saw themselves as Jesus at His baptism, awash in the water of new birth, born again from the Womb of the Holy Ghost - See *Ally Kateusx* amazing book *'Finding Holy Spirit Mother.'*

CHAPTER 10: APOCRYPHAL BOOK OF 'WISDOM OF SOLOMON' FROM THE OLD TESTAMENT

C.1 Here we have some more amazing verses from *'Wisdom of Solomon'*:

1.4 Because wisdom will not enter into a soul that devises evil, nor dwell in a body that is held in pledge by sin.

1.5 For a holy spirit of discipline will flee deceit, and will start away from thoughts that are without understanding, and will be put to confusion when unrighteousness hath come in.

1.6 For wisdom is a spirit that loveth man, and she will not hold a blasphemer guiltless for his lips; because God bears witness of his reins, and is a true overseer of his heart, and a hearer of his tongue:

1.7 Because the spirit of the Lord hath filled the world, and that which holds all things together hath knowledge of every voice.

WISDOM OF SOLOMON 6.12-22

12 Wisdom is radiant and fades not away; and easily is she beheld of them that love her, and found of them that seek her. She forestalled them that desire to know her, making herself first known. Wisdom Is glorious and never fades away. Yea, she is easily seen of them that love her and found of such as seek her.

13 She prevents them that desire her in making herself known unto them.

14 Whoso seeks her early shall have no great travail: for he shall find her sitting at his Doors.

15 To think therefore upon her is perfection of Wisdom: and whoso watches her shall quickly be without care.

16 For she goes about seeking such as are worthy of her, shews herself favourably unto them in the ways, and meets them in every thought.

17 For the very true beginning of her is the desire of discipline; and the care of discipline is love.

18 And love is the keeping of her laws and the giving heed to here laws is the assurance of incorruption.

19 And incorruption makes us close to 'God.

20 Therefore the desire of wisdom brings to a kingdom.

21 If your delight be in thrones and sceptres, O ye kings of the people, honour wisdom, that ye may reign for evermore.

22 As for Wisdom, what she is, and how she came up, I will tell you and will not hide mysteries from you: but seek her out from the beginning of her nativity, and bring the knowledge of her into light, and will not pass over the truth.

WISDOM OF SOLOMON CHAPTERS 7-9
CHAPTER 7.7-30

7 Wherefore I prayed, and understanding was given me: I called upon God, and the spirit of wisdom came to me.

8 I preferred her before sceptres and thrones, and esteemed riches nothing in comparison of her.

9 Neither compared I unto her any precious stone, because all gold in respect of her is as a little sand, and silver shall be counted as clay before her.

10 I loved her above health and beauty and chose to have her instead of light: for the light that cometh from her never goes out.

11 All good things together came to me with her, and innumerable riches in her hands.

12 And I rejoiced in them all, because wisdom goes before them: and I knew not that she was the mother of them.

13 I learned diligently and do communicate her liberally: I do not hide her riches.

14 For she is a treasure unto men that never fails: which they that use become the friends of God, being commended for the gifts that come from learning.

15 God has granted me to speak as I would, and to conceive as is meet for the things that are given me: because it is he that leadeth unto wisdom and directs the wise.

16 For in his hand are both we and our words; all wisdom also, and knowledge of workmanship.

17 For he hath given me certain knowledge of the things that are, namely, to know how the world was made, and the operation of the elements:

18 The beginning, ending, and midst of the times: the alterations of the turning of the sun, and the change of seasons:

19 The circuits of years, and the positions of stars:

C.2 These were also the very things revealed to Enoch of old concerning the Creation and the universe and what holds it all together.

20 The natures of living creatures, and the furies of wild beasts: the violence of winds, and the reasonings of men: the diversities of plants and the virtues of roots:

21 And all such things as are either secret or manifest, them I know.

22 For wisdom, which is the worker of all things, taught me: for in her is an understanding spirit holy, one only, manifold, subtill, lively, clear, undefiled, plain, not subject to hurt, loving the thing that is good quick, which cannot be letted (prevemted), ready to do good.

C.3 It would seem that some of the prophets were endowed with great wisdom to know of many things that in modern times even science knows nothing about because of their ungodliness and blatant unbelief in God.

23 Kind to man, steadfast, sure, free from care, having all power, overseeing all things, and going through all understanding, pure, and most subtill, spirits.

24 For wisdom is more moving than any motion: she passes and goes through all things by reason of her pureness.

25 For she is the breath of the power of God, and a pure influence flowing from the glory of the Almighty: therefore can no defiled thing fall into her.

26 For she is the brightness of the everlasting light, the unspotted mirror of the power of God, and the image of his goodness.

27 And being but one, she can do all things: and remaining in herself, she maketh all things new: and in all ages entering into holy souls, she maketh them friends of God, and prophets.

28 For God loveth none but him that dwelleth with wisdom.

29 For she is more beautiful than the sun, and above all the order of stars: being compared with the light, she is found before it.

30 For after this cometh night: but vice shall not prevail against wisdom.

APOCHRYPHA BOOK WISDOM CHAPTER 8 1-21

8.1 Wisdom reaches from one end to another mightily: and sweetly doth she order all things.

8.2 I loved her, and sought her out from my youth, I desired to make her my spouse, and I was a lover of her beauty.

C.4 Notice in Proverbs, that it states:-

Proverbs 18.22: 'Whoso finds a wife finds a good thing and obtains favour from the Lord'.

It also states in Proverbs about Wisdom:

Proverbs 8.35: 'For whoso finds me (Wisdom) finds life, and shall obtain favour of the Lord'.

WISDOM 8.3 'In that she is conversant with God, she magnifies her nobility: yea, the Lord of all things himself loved her.'

C.5 This verse shows that Wisdom is a very special being and normally when stated 'magnifies her nobility' this would mean like Esther of old, in the Old Testament who bettered Herself (by marrying the King Artaxerxes in around

470 BC) of the Persian Empire - and in this particular case Wisdom or also known as Holy Spirit Mother married Father God.

8.4 For she is privy to the mysteries of the knowledge of God, and a lover of his works.

8.5 If riches be a possession to be desired in this life; what is richer than wisdom, that worketh all things?

8.6 And if prudence work; who of all that are is a more cunning workman than she?

8.7 And if a man love righteousness her labours are virtues: for she teaches temperance and prudence, justice and fortitude: which are such things, as one can have nothing more profitable in their life.

C.6 Why do you suppose that the prophet writing this story wanted to be so close in spirit to the feminine spirit of Wisdom? Well, she was the Mother of Jesus the Christ, and in the Old Testament Jesus the Saviour of all mankind had not yet been born. It is stated about Jesus in the Book of Revelation that Jesus was the beginning of the Creation of God. Better said the beginning of God the Father and God the Mother. Jesus has the same sweetness of spirit as His Mother the Holy Spirit or also known as Wisdom (Sophia in Greek).

WISDOM 8.8 -21 If a man desire much experience, she knows things of old, and conjectures aright what is to come: she knows the subtilties of speeches, and can expound dark sentences: she foresees signs and wonders, and the events of seasons and times.

8.9 Therefore I purposed to take her to me to live with me, knowing that she would be a counsellor of good things, and a comfort in cares and grief.

8.10 For her sake I shall have estimation among the multitude, and honour with the elders, though I be young.

8.11 I shall be found of a quick conceit in judgment, and shall be admired in the sight of great men.

8.12 When I hold my tongue, they shall bide my leisure, and when I speak, they shall give good ear unto me: if I talk much, they shall lay their hands upon their mouth.

8.13 Moreover by the means of her I shall obtain immortality and leave behind me an everlasting memorial to them that come after me.

C.7 This is truly an amazing verse for the Old Testament. It is stating something from the New Testament how that the Holy Spirit Mother took good care of God's children. Those who received Jesus as their Saviour and were thus saved souls. This verse 13 is describing Wisdom in the Old Testament as feminine and as Mother as is also the Holy Spirit Mother described in the New Testament. This must mean that the Holy Spirit and Wisdom are one and the same, being feminine and Mother God in the Trinity. Just amazing!

8.14 I shall set the people in order, and the nations shall be subject unto me.

C.8 This last verse sounds like the future after Jesus Christ, the Son of the Holy Spirit Mother has returned at the 2nd coming and during the time of the Golden Age of the Millennium when the Holy Spirit Mother along with her Son Jesus will rule over the nations of the world and Satan will no longer be the 'god of this world' but will have been cast into the bottomless Pit for 1000 years.

8.15 Horrible tyrants shall be afraid, when they do but hear of me; I shall be found good among the multitude, and valiant in war.

C.9 It sounds like a change is coming in the future as the Merchants and the rich and rulers of today will one day lose their power and riches and the spirit of love and gentleness take over and the Devil's people will no longer be around the earth.

8.16 After I am come into mine house, I will repose myself with her: for her conversation hath no bitterness; and to live with her hath no sorrow, but mirth and joy.

8.17 Now when I considered these things in myself, and pondered them in my heart, how that to be allied unto wisdom is immortality;

C.10 This verse seems to be saying that Wisdom gives those dedicated to her immortality? How is that possible? We become immortal by receiving her Son Jesus as the Messiah and saviour of our souls which will give us immortality. It is very interesting how his prophet was taking about immortality of souls in the Old Testament and long before the Messiah came to earth.

8.18 And great pleasure it is to have her friendship; and in the works of her hands are infinite riches; and in the exercise of conference with her, prudence; and in talking with her, a good report; I went about seeking how to take her to me.

8.19 For I was a witty child and had a good spirit.

8.20 Yea rather, being good, I came into a body undefiled.

8.21 Nevertheless, when I perceived that I could not otherwise obtain her, except God gave her me; and that was a point of wisdom also to know whose gift she was; I prayed unto the Lord, and besought him, and with my whole heart I said.

APOCHRYPHA: WISDOM 9.4,9-18

9.4 Give me wisdom, that sits by thy throne; and reject me not from among thy children:

C.11 Here it is stating that Mother God sits right next to God the Father on His throne as she is clearly His wife. Jesus the Messiah was there first born Son.

9.9 And wisdom was with thee: which knows thy works, and She was present when thou made the world, and knew what was acceptable in thy sight, and right in thy commandments.

9.10 O send her out of thy holy heavens, and from the throne of thy glory, that being present she may labour with me, that I may know what is pleasing unto thee.

C.12 Is it just possible that the Holy Spirit Mother in talking to the prophet or in being with him a lot of the time according to Proverbs she has a lot of her maidens of wisdom. Is it possible in the case of this prophet that she sent one of her maidens of Wisdom to be with the prophet as he desired wisdom to live with him like a wife I suppose. At least in spirit.

Proverbs 9.1-3 Wisdom hath built her house, she hath hewn out her seven pillars: She hath killed her beasts; she hath mingled her wine; she hath also furnished her table. She hath sent forth her maidens: (Other female spirits of Wisdom)

9.11 For she knows and understands all things, and she shall lead me soberly in my doings, and preserve me in her power.

9.12 So shall my works be acceptable, and then shall I judge thy people righteously, and be worthy to sit in my father›s seat.

9.13 For what man is he that can know the counsel of God? or who can think what the will of the Lord is?

9.14 For the thoughts of mortal men are miserable, and our devices are but uncertain.

9.15 For the corruptible body presses down the soul, and the earthy tabernacle weighs down the mind that muses upon many things.

9.16 And hardly do we guess aright at things that are upon earth, and with labour do we find the things that are before us: but the things that are in heaven who hath searched out?

9.17 And thy counsel who hath known, except thou give wisdom, and send thy Holy Spirit from above?

9.18 For so the ways of them which lived on the earth were reformed, and men were taught the things that are pleasing unto thee, and were saved through wisdom.

CHAPTER 11: Holy Spirit Mother

1) She is the wife of Father God

2) Jesus is their Son

3) God created man and woman in His & Her Image.

GENESIS 1.26 And God said, 'Let **us** make man in our image, after our likeness: and let them have dominion over the fish of the sea, and over the fowl of the air, and over the cattle, and over all the earth, and over every creeping thing that creeps upon the earth.

C.1 In other words in His and Her likeness as He stated to His partner the Holy Spirit Mother:

GENESIS 1.27 So God created man in his *own image*, in the image of God created he him; *male and female* created he them.

GENESIS 1.28 And God blessed them, and God said unto them, *'Be fruitful, and multiply*, and replenish the earth, and subdue it: and have dominion over the fish of the sea, and over the fowl of the air, and over every living thing that moves upon the earth'.

C.2 Who was God talking to unless it was *a female* – His *divine wife* -The *Holy Spirit Mother* –

She is also known as *Divine Wisdom/Sophia -The Divine Feminine*

C.3 As is made very clear: men and women were created to work together as a couple and to have a family.

C.4 The physical life that we have on earth seems to be divided into different time zones of experience or Creation.

1) Conceived
2) Born
3) Baby
4) Small Child
5) Child
6) Teenager
7) Older Teenager
8) Young Adult
9) Adult
10) Middle-aged Adult
11) Mature adult
12) Old person
13) Aged person/very old person.

We pass through these different stages and it would seem that each one of them is very different as to the new things that we are supposed to learn during that phase of life. What is important is that we have the best teachers during those early years whilst growing up. I am not talking about intellectual teachers but spiritual teachers who believe in Jesus and God.

C.5 Personally, I did not count my life to have truly begun until I got saved at the age of 20. I went to the best all boys boarding schools until 18 and then went to university but I felt totally empty inside as though all I had done so far was pointless and had all been forced upon me by my family who meant me well but were atheists in practice. I didn't come to know God until I was an adult or stage 8) in the above-mentioned chart. The tragedy in modern times is that most people don't get truly saved in this present life.

C.6 The best teacher is Holy Spirit Mother, and she delights in teaching those who love Her Son Jesus the Messiah.

C.7 It is tragic when the baby is not born into new life but dies before it can even be born and given life. This is reflected in the fact that there are over 140,000,000 births; 73,000,000 abortions every year. 60,000,000 other deaths. Shockingly, experts from the USA have stated that at this very moment.

Author: That would imply that currently we have 4 times the number of deaths as in the pre-Covid times. How is that most don't even notice this eugenics operation going on? Have we lost many people in the past 4 years? The answer is YES apparently!

CHAPTER 12: SOPHIA GREEK WORD FOR WISDOM

Here is what others say about SOFIA or WISDOM the Greek Goddess with my comments afterwards:

C.1 The feminine name Sophia is the Greek word for wisdom. In looking up the word SOPHIA it shows a remarkable number of famous people with that name from many different countries through thousands of years since the Old Grecian empire which started in 333 BC and seems to have been adopted by celebrities, queens and princesses from all over the world.

Sophia, also spelled **Sofia**, is a feminine given name, from Greek Σοφία, *Sophía*, "Wisdom". Other forms include Sophie, Sophy, and **Sofie**.: Sophia (given name) - Wikipedia

Sophia: Goddess of Wisdom & God's Wife

Who is Sophia? Literally she is Wisdom, because the Greek word *Sophia* means "wisdom" in English. More than that, Sophia is the Wisdom of Deity. She has been revered as the Wise Bride of Solomon by Jews, as the Queen of Wisdom and War (Athena) by Greeks, and as the Holy Spirit of Wisdom by Christians

Seminary - Sophia: Goddess of Wisdom & God's Bride

Wisdom Personified in Various Beliefs

Hebrew Tradition: In the Book of Proverbs, wisdom is personified as a woman, reflecting aspects of Sophia.

Christian Gnosticism: Texts like the *Pistis Sophia* portray her seeking redemption, guided by Jesus Christ. The Valentinian Gnostics emphasize her restoration through the intervention of the Savior, often identified with the Logos or Christ.: Sophia in Gnosticism: Goddess of the Divine Feminine | Gaia

Spirituality in Mature Women

Sophia is the Christian spirit of spiritual wisdom in women's spiritual circles, in which she is viewed as the Divine Feminine. Sophia's identity is hidden in the Old Testament by references to her in the lowercase word "wisdom." She was a part of the Judeo-Christian heritage of the West, but forgotten within a monotheistic, patriarchal religion that denies feminine divinity.

Sophia was a major figure in the beliefs of first-century Gnostic Christians, who were denounced as heretics and persecuted in the fourth century. Thankfully, copies of the Gnostic Gospels were found in the mid-twentieth century, hidden away in the Nag Hammadi desert in Egypt. It is very important for women to be aware that the worship and knowledge of feminine divinity have disappeared because the patriarchy is based upon negating women's spiritual authority. The historical inferior status of women and the suppression of the goddess are related, just as the dominant position of men is related to monotheism.

Enlightened women know that men altered the Bible and got rid of any books of it that mentioned women in positions of power. There is no word for goddess in Hebrew. This non designation led to non-recognition. The elimination of the goddess was required by monotheism. When the Bible speaks of "false gods" people can miss the point that God was eradicating worship of the goddess, making women abominations and cursed.

In Genesis, there is one Father God, who is supreme and exists from the beginning. He has no lineage, family, or spouse. Yet the promised land of Canaan already belonged to goddess worshiping people. After the land and people were conquered, the prophets were against Asherah, Anath and Ashtoreth, whom were women, and goddesses! Asherah was the Semitic name of the great goddess, the "Mother of all Wisdom."

How do we characterize wisdom, and thus explore Sophia? Webster's dictionary tells us that knowledge is the condition of apprehending fact, or cognition, while wisdom is the ability to discern inner qualities; in my words, reconnecting to that which is present beneath surface appearances.

Language -wise, wisdom started out as feminine in the Hebrew word hokhma, the Greek word Sophia, and the Latin word Sapientia. Wisdom became a neuter gender to the Greeks, called Pneuma, personified as a dove, the animal strongly associated with Sophia. As language moved to a more masculine expression of God, so did the image of Goddess move, from a vibrant creatrix to a passive adjunct or receptacle for the male seed. In her role as feminine divine, Sophia is woven into goddess tradition over much of the world. She appears to have emerged as a central figure in the Christian philosophical movement called Gnosticism, likely originating in ancient Rome and Persia, a mystical sect embracing individual realization of the divine through ecstatic inner experience. This alone tells us much of the nature of Sophia: she is the inner knowing, rather than the knowledge gained from the outside world.

C.2 SUMMARY: Steve (Author of this book) In studying what others say about **SOPHIA** they largely see her as a goddess who fell at some point and was later redeemed. I do not see her that way at all. I believe that Sophia which means Wisdom in Greek is the name of a much higher entity and that Sophia is talking about the Holy Spirit Mother the very wife of God the Father who are both the parents of Jesus the Messiah.

C.3 The ancient Israelites killed those who worshipped the ancient goddesses like Astaroth because they were evil and getting the ancient Israelites to worship idols to which even Solomon ended up falling for.

C.4 I believe that the reason the Holy Spirt Mother has been deliberately hidden for almost 1700 years now in making her out to be part of an all-masculine Trinity is simple.

Many of the past religionists simply don't like the feminine side to rule over men as they are afraid that what happened in Pre-Flood times might happen again. What was that you may ask?

C.5 They are afraid that men could be replaced by *fallen angels* or *demons* being with the women or their wives in place of themselves. Since the Tower of Babel mankind has been subjugating the women into 2nd or 3rd place.

C.6 It is basically fear that has caused the problem in hiding away the truth of the Holy Spirit Mother.

C.7 Woman need to know that they do have an eternal Mother who cares for them and that She is married to God the Father. She is an eternal being and that Jesus is their Son who become creator of the physical realm.

C.8 I think that Jesus was given a lot of help and advice from His parents during the whole Creation of the physical realm.

C.9 I would say that it is essential to know that Holy Spirit Mother herself would want us to emphasize her Son Jesus at the present time more than herself as we all need Jesus to get saved spiritually and that is the most important thing to learn in this life.

C.10 I am sure that whatever we have not yet learned here on earth will yet be shown to us in the spirit world when we die. God loves each one of us very much and he simply wants us all to get saved and come to be his children whom He can both love and take good care of.

C.11 However, although the above is certainly true I do think it is a tragedy that the knowledge of the Holy Spirit Mother has been deliberately hidden for 1700 years. Why? Because suppressing the feminine side has created an imbalance. God made things to be 50% male and 50% female both in the spirit world and the physical.

C.12 Sadly, mysticism is often just a way to minimize the very great importance of Salvation through Jesus Christ the Saviour and circumvent this truth by another way of 'self-awareness and meditation.

C.13 Please don't get me wrong, as I think there are a lot of good things in meditation and meditating on the positive, but you need to make sure that you are protected by knowing Jesus and His salvation by grace as unfortunately, we all have a strong enemy called Satan who is a Deceiver.

C.14 When you have Jesus in your heart then you don't need to be afraid of anything or anyone. What you do have to do is to daily read the Bible and especially the 4 Gospels as to what the Saviour taught us in how to live our lives. Once you know the Bible please also read the Apocrypha books which fill in more details.

CHAPTER 13: HOLY SPIRIT MOTHER AND THE BIRTH OF A NEW SOUL

C.1 Spiritually speaking, it is very sad for God when so many people on earth never get 'born again' in the way that Jesus the Son of Man explained in his famous discourse of *John chapter 3* when He was talking to the learned leader of the Jews know as Nicodemus.

John Chapter 3

There was a man of the Pharisees, named Nicodemus, a ruler of the Jews:

The same came to Jesus by night, and said unto him, Rabbi, we know that thou art a teacher come from God: for no man can do these miracles that thou doest, except God be with him.

Jesus answered and said unto him, Verily, verily, I say unto thee, 'Except a man be born again, he cannot see the kingdom of God.' Nicodemus saith unto him, 'How can a man be born when he is old? can he enter the second time into his mother's womb, and be born?' Jesus answered, Verily, verily, I say unto thee, 'Except a man be born of water and of the Spirit, he cannot enter into the kingdom of God'. That which is born of the flesh is flesh; and that which is born of the Spirit is spirit. Marvel not that I said unto thee, Ye must be born again.

C.2 This verse is incredible as it reveals something profound. It is stating that one has to be born physically and spiritually. It says that spiritually one is born again by the Spirit of Mother God as She is the feminine in the Godhead - the Mother. 'Except a man be born of water and *of the Spirit*, he cannot enter into the kingdom of God'. That which is born of the flesh is flesh; and that which is *born of the Spirit* is spirit. Marvel not that I said unto thee, *Ye must be born again*.

C.3 Holy Spirit Mother is described as a *mother* in many ancient scriptures from the Apocryphal books. When a person asks Jesus into their hearts, it is the Holy Spirit Mother who is involved in the spiritual birth of that person as they become a new person completely. The Prayer for getting saved is very simple. First one has to confess ones need for God and for Jesus his Son. We confess our need for God and ask Him to forgive us our sins. We then ask Jesus the Son of God to come into our hearts and to save us from our sins. We are normally quite desperate with God in our plea and then Jesus does come into our hearts through the power of the Holy Spirit Mother re-birthing us into a new life in Spirit.

The Holy Spirit Mother is involved when a new soul is born, as she has to do with all 'births'. In becoming a disciple for Christ one has to ask for the anointing of the Holy Spirit which is a special anointing given by God to His saints to enable them to have the power and wisdom to be a witness for Jesus about simple Salvation.

It can be an ecstatic experience, as it was for me, when I got saved at 19 years old.

C.4 That is the problem with the organized churches - they are far too complicated when it comes to simple Salvation - as anyone can get saved and not just goodie-goodie church people. Any honest sinner can come to Christ and be born again by the Holy Spirit Mother. It was the Catholic church which took away the simple knowledge that the Holy Spirit is feminine and the Mother of all of us.

C.5 Why do I say the expression 'goodie-goodie church people'? Because from my experience of visiting different churches most of those people are not actually saved, as they don't believe in Salvation by Grace as according to Titus 3.5 but think that it is their good works that will earn their way to heaven. But they are not sure if they are saved or not by their own works!

Titus 3.5 Not by works of righteousness which we have done, but according to his mercy he saved us, by the washing of regeneration, and renewing of the *Holy Ghost*.

C.6 The point is none of us can save ourselves by our good works. Jesus died on the cross that we might be saved. Nobody else can save us and certainly not ourselves. What is it that stops so many from getting truly 'saved by Grace'?

We cannot work our way to heaven by our so-called 'good works' – that is Satan's counterfeit! It is all a gift of God.

C.7 St Paul argued with St Peter on this very point stating that the old law could not save you but only the Grace of God through Jesus the Messiah.

Galatians 2.21 "I do not frustrate the grace of God: for if righteousness *come* by the law, then Christ is dead in vain."

John 3.16 For God so love the world that He gave His only Begotten Son that whosoever believes in Him should not perish but have everlasting life.

Ephesians 2-8-9 For by grace are ye saved through faith; and that not of yourselves: it is the gift of God: Not of works, lest any man should boast.

Titus 3.5 "Not by works of righteousness which we have done, but according to his mercy he saved us, by the washing of regeneration, and renewing of the Holy Ghost;"

C.8 Why is it that most church people are not actually saved? Because they hold to 'religious traditions' like the Pharisees in the time of Jesus instead of embracing the Word of God which is very simple: 'Except Ye be converted and become as a little child, Ye cannot enter into the kingdom of God' Religious people often only have the 'letter of the law' and not the real Salvation offered by Jesus Christ. It all depends on what is your motive to begin with!

C.9 There seems to be Satan's imitation of the true 'Born again' experience that does not involve the Holy Spirit Mother That is why Satan cooked up the idea of the 'all masculine Trinity' in 364 AD at Laodicea. It is some sort of 'works trip' where people become more dedicated to the church or church building or other icon of man's false religions but not Christ.

C.10 I think that many people join churches in order to 'better themselves', but not because they genuinely are saved or even want to get saved. The 'Goodie Goodies' think they can better themselves through religion and often they become very self-righteous about going to church etc but they are not willing to truly 'forsake all' as in Luke 14.33 and follow in Jesus footsteps as Jesus commanded His disciples to do 'Go Ye into all the world and preach the Gospel unto every creature. In other words, Jesus told His disciples to go into all the world and tell others how to get saved by asking Jesus into their hearts.

Luke 14.33 So likewise, whosoever he be of you that forsaketh not all that he hath, he cannot be my disciple.

WHAT ABOUT BECOMING A DISCIPLE FOR CHRIST?

C.11 Most church people are simply not willing to make the sacrifice to give up their own lives and follow Jesus in humility and sincerity and spend their lives talking to others about 'getting saved' which is the most important job in the world.

Mark 16.15 'Go Ye therefore into all the world and preach the gospel unto every creature.'

C.12 The *Holy Spirit Mother is the Comforter* who longs to comfort people to come to Jesus in humility. The Holy Spirit Mother is not around the proud religious people. God's Spirit is gentle. She is loving and kind as well as merciful. She states however that there are certain behaviours that she abhors - one is Pride and another is arrogance.

C.13 That is often the sin of the church people, as they go around condemning others instead of humbly loving others. Jesus stated in Matthew 7.

Matthew 7.1-3 Judge not, that ye be not judged. For with what judgment ye judge, ye shall be judged: and with what measure ye mete, it shall be measured to you again. ^{3}And why behold thou the mote that is in thy brother's eye, but consider not the beam that is in thine own eye?

IMPORTANCE OF GOD'S WORD

C.14 From my experience, church people don't' seem to make progress in their 'walk with the Lord' In general - they don't read their Bibles, and yet they think that they have the right to judge others?! It is the Bible that helps us to walk in the Truth and helps to treat others with consideration. Only God's Spirit working through His Word can help each one of us to behave in a godly manner. Did you know that 70% of pastors in the US Church system don't use the Bible anymore. How can others follow the true Christianity just by going to those churches?

Galatians 5.22-23 For the fruit of the Spirit is Love, Joy, Peace, Longsuffering, Gentleness, Goodness, Faith, Meekness Temperance against such there is no law.

C.15 Author: Disclaimer: I also know that, of course, there are good pastors of churches and there are good congregations who do love Jesus very much and do help a lot in their communities. The important thing as a Christian is to love Jesus and desire to love and help others to also know about Salvation by Grace.

SALVATION

I challenge you, that if you have not already prayed to receive Jesus into your heart, so that you can have eternal life, & be guaranteed an eternal place in Heaven, then please do so immediately, to keep you safe from what is soon coming upon the earth!

Revelations 3.20 "Behold, I stand at the door and knock, if any man hear my voice, and open the door, I will come in to him and live with him and him with me".

John 3.36.

"He who believes on the Son of God has eternal life."

That means right now! Once saved, you are eternally saved, and here is a very simple prayer to help you to get saved:

"Dear Jesus, 'Please, come into my heart, forgive me all of my sins, give me eternal life, and fill me with your Holy Spirit. Please help me to love others and to read the Word of God in Jesus name, Amen'."

Once you've prayed that little prayer sincerely, then you are guaranteed a wonderful future in Heaven for eternity with your creator and loved ones.

1 John 4.16 "For God is Love"

Your Salvation does not depend on you going to church, and your good works.

Titus 3.5 "Not by works of righteousness which we have done, but according to His mercy he *saved* us".

Your salvation only depends on receiving Christ as your saviour, not on church or religion!

John 6.38 "He that comes unto Me, I will in no wise cast out"- Jesus

John 3.3 Jesus explained that unless you become as a child, you won't even understand the Kingdom of Heaven.

C.16 Do you have enough love to teach others about Jesus and His Word?

CHAPTER 14: ACTS OF THOMAS & ODES OF SOLOMON

C.1 More about Holy Spirit Mother

Teachings of Silvanus (1st to 3rd century) found in Nag Hammadi in Coptic and originally in Greek.

QUOTE: 'My child, return to your first Father, God, and Wisdom, your Mother, from whom you came into being from the beginning. Return, that you might fight against all of your enemies, the power of the adversary.

C.2 The Holy Spirit as Mother in the *Acts of Thomas*

The *Acts of Thomas* is an anonymous work which was originally written in Syriac sometime around 220 A D. It also survives in a Greek translation which "shows less signs of revision and appears to preserve a more primitive [i.e. an earlier] form of the text." The Holy Spirit is plainly called Mother several times in the surviving Syriac, and even more so in the Greek translation.

Some suggest that the *Acts of Thomas* reflects gnostic beliefs or the beliefs of the heterodox Valentinians. Others suggest it simply reflects the beliefs of early Syriac Christianity. Whatever the case, like the other Apocryphal Acts, this work has a strong emphasis on celibacy as desirable for a pious Christian life.

At the end of an enigmatic song sung by the apostle Judas Thomas in the First Act, is this line.

And they have glorified and praised with the living Spirit, the Father of truth and the Mother of Wisdom.

C.3 In the Second Act, after the apostle baptised king Gundaphorus and his brother Gad and anointed them with oil, there is this invocation.

Come, holy name of the Messiah that is above every name.

Come, power of the Most High, and the compassion that is perfect.

Come, gift (Greek: *charisma*) of the Most High.

Come, compassionate Mother.

Come, communion of the male

Come, she who reveals the hidden mysteries.

Come, Mother of the seven houses, that thy rest may be in the eighth house.

Come, Elder (masculine in the Greek) of the five members: mind, thought, reflection, consideration, reason;

Communicate with these young men.

Come, Holy Spirit, and cleanse their minds and hearts The Holy Spirit as Mother in Early Syriac Texts - Marg Mowczko

C.4 In the Fourth Act, the apostle speaks to Jesus and says,

"We glorify and praise you and your invisible Father and your Holy Spirit, the Mother of all creation." (section 39 from the Greek)

"We glorify you and we exalt through you your exalted Father, who is not seen, and the Holy Spirit that broods over all created things." (section 39, Kijn's translation from the Syriac).

C.5 In the Fifth Act, in a prayer said before the apostle shares the eucharist, there is another invocation.

Come, O perfect compassion,

Come, O communion of the male,

Come, she who knows the mysteries of him that is chosen,

Come, she who has a part in all the combats of the noble champion (athlete),

Come, the silence that reveals the great things of the whole greatness,

Come, she who manifests the hidden things and makes the unspeakable things plain, the holy dove that bears the twin young,

Come, the hidden Mother,

Come, she who is shown in her deeds and gives joy and rest to those who are joined to her:

Come and communicate with us in this eucharist which we celebrate in your name and in the love-feast where we have gathered together at your calling. (section 50 from the Greek)

C.6 In the Fifth Act, after the family of Siphor are baptised, a prayer is said for them which includes these lines.

"..we invoke upon you the name of the Mother of the unspeakable mystery of the hidden powers and authorities; we invoke upon you the name of Jesus ..." (section 133)

C.7 "Mother" is also mentioned in the enigmatic Hymn of the Pearl (or, Hymn of the Soul) contained in the *Acts of Thomas*. This may be another reference to the Holy Spirit. (section 109.41)

Maternal Imagery for God in the *Odes of Solomon*

C.8 The *Odes of Solomon* are 42 lyric poems that were written in the late first century, or sometime during the second century, by a Jewish-Christian author or school. The Odes survive in both Syriac and Greek. The most complete surviving collection is in Syriac, but it seems at least a few of the Odes were originally written in Greek.

ODE 28 was written when the author was being persecuted but the lines about the Holy Spirit are especially beautiful.

As the wings of doves over their nestlings, and the mouths of their nestlings towards their mouths, so also are the wings of the Spirit over my heart.

My heart continually refreshes itself and leaps for joy, like the babe who leaps for joy in his mother's womb. [...]

And immortal life embraced me and kissed me.

And from that life is the Spirit which is within me. And it cannot die because it is life.

ODE 36 begins with a couple of statements about the Spirit using feminine language in the Syriac.

C.9 The word for "spirit, breath, wind" in Hebrew (*ruach*) and in Aramaic (*rucha*), including Syriac, is usually grammatically feminine.

Some information about Syriac:

C.10 "The seven houses referred to are the planetary spheres through which Sophia [the Spirit] descends: the eighth, the ogdoad, is the place of rest above them, the heavenly bridechamber. The eighth sphere.

C.11 THE DOVE OF THE HOLY SPIRIT

ODES OF SOLOMON 24 1 'The Dove fluttered over the Messiah, because He was her head; and she sang over Him and her voice was heard'. It would appear that the **Dove** represents the **Holy Spirit Mother** who is with Christ and this verse is similar to a New Testament verse.

Luke 3.32 And the Holy Ghost descended in a bodily shape like a **dove** upon him, and a voice came from heaven, which said, 'Thou art my beloved Son; in thee I am well pleased'.

In the Bible the word **dove** is mentioned many times in different connotations:

The harbinger of peace to Noah.

Genesis 8:8 Genesis 8:10-12.

Genesis 8.8 "And he stayed yet other seven days; and sent forth the *dove*; which returned not again unto him anymore."

[10] He waited seven more days and again sent out the *dove* from the ark.

[11] When the *dove* returned to him in the evening, there in its beak was a freshly plucked olive leaf! Then Noah knew that the water had receded from the earth.

[12] He waited seven more days and sent the *dove* out again, but this time it did not return to him.

The emblem of purity

Psalm 68.13 Though ye have lien among the pots yet shall ye be as the wings of a *dove* covered with silver, and her feathers with yellow gold.

A symbol of the Holy Spirit

Genesis 1.2 And the earth was without form, and void; and darkness was upon the face of the deep. And the *Spirit of God* moved upon the face of the waters.

Matthew 3:16

[16] And Jesus, when he was baptized, went up straightway out of the water: and, lo, the heavens were opened unto him, and he saw the *Spirit* of God descending like a *dove*, and lighting upon him:

[17] And lo a voice from heaven, saying, This is my beloved Son, in whom I am well pleased.

John 1:32 "And John bare record, saying, I saw the Spirit descending from heaven like a dove, and it abode upon him.").

CHAPTER 15: THE IMPORTANCE OF MARRIAGE – God Is the One Who Designed Marriage

C.1 This word marriage means commitment. 'Stay together' through thick and thin. Marriage is a lot more than just sex, although sex can be beautiful and an important part, especially when you are young. Not everyone would agree about this statement though. I would state marriage is also caring for each other which normally becomes more self-evident as we get older. As in the old-fashioned values when one initially gets married and commits oneself to another person: 'In sickness and in health'. 'For richer or poorer'.

NOTE: The words "in sickness and in health," typically followed by "till death do us part," are a central component of the marriage vows in many religions and cultures. The origin of the phrase is usually attributed to Thomas Cramner, who adapted the terminology in the original Book of Common Prayer published in 1549.

C.2 The great importance of the feminine side The feminine side often tells us 'men' to 'restrain' from doing dumb things. Good to be married I say. The feminine side is much more intuitive, which the masculine side tends to both ignore and minimize.

C.3 The feminine side tends to be more merciful and concerned and caring in many cases. God gave women more emotions than men for a good reason.

C.4 Sadly, I know that there is too much so-called 'women's lib' with women thinking that they have to behave the same way as a man - which is not how things are supposed to be. Men and women are created different from each other but both are equally valuable.

C.5 Marriage and having children The Population is actually decreasing in many countries. It is causing a lot of trouble in modern society as now 54% of women in modern times are not even married by the age of 30! Thirty years ago, there were only 18% of women still unmarried at 30 years of age. Another recent tragedy in Western society is that many women are starting menopause very early between 30 to 35, and so the population of the nations is now quickly receding in the West and Japan .Apparently all nations are now seeing a rapid decrease in their populations.

C.6 What is happening in society is certainly not natural and certainly it is not the will of God and Mother God. The facts are that 'The Western society' will come to an end in 20-30 years due to the lack of having both babies and children. If men and women would simply look at how things are and change their ways perhaps the Western society would not have to collapse in the year future. Women are telling me that women are not having children anymore because life is just too expensive now in 2025 here in the UK. What a sad state of affairs!

C.7 In contrast many would say what about all those who have dedicated themselves to God in this life and yet have chosen to be eunuchs, whether nuns or monks or other devoted religious people. Yes, Jesus did talk about this topic. Jesus does mention that some people choose to be celibate, and some do so for the Kingdom of God's sake,

Matthew 19.12 'For there are some eunuchs, which were so born from their mother's womb: and there are some eunuchs, which were made eunuchs of men: and there be eunuchs, which have made themselves eunuchs for the kingdom of heaven's sake. He that is able to receive it, let him receive it.'

C.8 Nevertheless, God never intended us to minimize both marriage and having children as that was His very first commandment to mankind 'Be fruitful and multiply'. I am convinced that motherhood is something that most women were supposed to experience and most men were supposed to be fathers.

C.9 The fact that the Catholic church caused so much celibacy to spring up since the year 364 AD and the council of Laodicea. The very time when the Holy Spirit being feminine was altered to masculine and the amazing Books of Enoch were also banned.

C.10 That one event in time has taken away so much of the true feminine values. The feminine values have very often been sissified and put down and minimized and the harsh tough unloving bullying spirit has been allowed to rule instead - the demonic side of things.

C.11 Look of all the incessant brutality of man's wars and oppression of innocent peoples and the slaughter of the innocents! Not to mention all the sexual perversions that have been encouraged by those religions that suppress the feminine side of things.

C.12 The feminine side of things is certainly not a weakness but actually a strength to everyone.

C.13 Unfortunately, since this current world is largely run by devils and the rich doing their biddings, they don't like the facts such as the Holy Spirit Mother being feminine, as it gets in the way of all of their perversions and oppressions of others, including the innocent. Marriage is being minimized.

C.14 As in regard to the choice of marriage or celibacy I would mention that things can be a certain way when we are young, and yet when we get older or even old we could end up alone for quite some time and no longer have sexual relationships with anyone. Maybe our mate died or they are too ill. So, there are different stages during life and celibacy could also be one of those stages. Whatever we suffer here is because this life is only temporal, and things don't last. Look forward to the eternal world and eternal life where there is no death nor sorrow or crying neither is there any more pain.

Revelation 21.4-6 And God shall wipe away all tears from their eyes; and there shall be no more death, neither sorrow, nor crying, neither shall there be any more pain: for the former things are passed away. And he that sat upon the throne said, Behold, I make all things new. And he said unto me, 'Write: for these words are true and faithful'. And he said unto me, It is done. I am Alpha and Omega, the beginning and the end. I will give unto him that is athirst of the fountain of the water of life freely.

C.15 God's perfect plan is for young people to marry and have children according to God's original great plan for Adam and Eve. His commandment to them was: 'Be fruitful and multiply' There is normally only a small window of time for having babies and children from the woman being around 22 to 40 in general.

C.16 What about relationships once we get to Heaven. Do people marry or are they given in marriage? According to Jesus we will be as the angels of God and *not* given in marriage.

NB However, Jesus in stating this did not say that those in the spirit world don't have sex.

C.17 If the Fallen angels could come down and have sex with the women on the earth in Pre-Flood times then this proves that there must by deduction be female angels in heaven. Do angels of God have sex? - See Genesis 6

C.18 If we will be like the angels, then we also will be able to have sex. *Without male and female interaction sexually, there would be no future races* either in the physical world or the much vaster spiritual world.

C.19 Sex is important to creation. Look at the nature. This is why Satan hid the facts about the Holy Spirit Mother being feminine back in 364 AD. It is tragic that religions have a taboo concerning sex when it was supposed to be a natural and godly thing in the right relationships. It is tragic that young people in the West are not taught any godly values in the normal schools and universities.

The modern way of thinking 'anything goes' and promiscuity do not build good marriages and relationships and do not provide a secure atmosphere for having a family.

C.20 The big problem is that Satan has gotten into the 'mixture' from the beginning of Creation. Satan hates sex and procreation and tries his hardest to condemn all sexuality that he has no control over. Satan controls all the perversions and things that God would not agree with. However, normal sex is not a crime.

C.21 Sex is extreme pleasure (well it is supposed to be) and a way of expressing love in the correct relationships. It is important that sex like any other pleasure is not overrun by excess or even demonic activity due to perversions. Sex is a beautiful activity that results in babies. Without the babies, human-beings cannot continue. That is a fact. So, motherhood is extremely important and should be honoured by all.

C.22 How to distinguish between love and lust? Love is concern for another person. Lust is what you can take from a person without giving anything back and can become demonic.

C.23 Old fashioned marriage is a good idea. In my opinion, having families is also a very good idea. I see a world today where people no longer get married. In the Western world I see a world where the babies are no longer being born. 54% of woman in the West are not married by the age of 30 these days.

C.24 Did you know that ½ of babies born today are aborted. It is very sad time indeed. Motherhood is largely *not* honoured in this present world. However, I can tell you this much that in Heaven Motherhood is highly honoured.

C.25 Satan has been the enemy of both women and sex since the very beginning of God's Creation. First, he managed to entice and then seduce Eve into having sex with him. See my book Secrets of Enoch Insights. She then conceived Cain. This son of Satan later produced the licentious daughters of Cain in around 300 years after Creation who seduced the Fallen Angels and together, they produced the Giants.

C.26 The giants were made to fight against each other and to destroy each other according to the 1st Book of Enoch. When the giants died, they descended down to the netherworld in the centre of our hollow planet.

C.28 After the Great Flood according to the Hebrew book of Jubilees the Giants came back as demons which brought the sicknesses to our planet. Those perverse demons were homosexual in their being. How did that happen? Well, when the giants were first created, the Fallen angels made a very big miscalculation.

C.29 You see in the case of the Fallen angels when they didn't acknowledge the Holy Spirit Mother as co-Creation with God the Father then you will leave out the feminine side in the birth of all your children. Somehow the Fallen angels could only transmit male genes to the human woman partners. Why? Now that is the question. Maybe the point is that angelic DNA was not designed to mix with human DNA and so something went wrong with the mixture which created massive giants and also *only male giants*.

C.30 Author: This is my theory: As a result, *all the giants were male* and there were no females. This drove the giants wild and they started to perv on each other. This is why there is such perversion on our planet today especially among the 'rich and educated'. I know that it is hard to recognize some of the above-mentioned matters.

C.31 Just remember what Satan himself said to Jesus when our Saviour was visiting our planet '*This world is delivered unto me and I give to whom I will.*'

Luke 4.6 And the devil said unto him, All this power will I give thee, and the glory of them: for that is *delivered unto me*; and to whomsoever I will I give it.

How on earth did God's original Creation of the physical realms end up in the hands of Satan? Well, that goes back to the Fall of Man. The fall of man was not sex but disobeying God's commandments and listening to Satan the snake or the dragon. God gave man choice to do Good or Evil and unfortunately in most cases the evil was chosen by man in the past as it is today.

C.32 First of all, we have to explain that female angels exist in heaven, and I have seen some of them upon occasion. They are incredibly beautiful and have an extremely caring spirit. When I first saw one of them it made me feel like a 2-year-old child by comparison. I now believe that I saw a glimpse of the Holy Spirit Mother rather than female angels, because of how it affected me. In a split-second of that amazing experience I felt so loved. Personally, seeing female angels: She was very concerned about me. I saw her around 4 times, and suddenly I was in the intensive care at the hospital receiving 4 blood transfusions for extreme anaemia. That was back in 2010.

C.33 I can personally tell you that female angels do exist. Of course, sexual relationships between a man and woman or even between angels or even other heavenly beings is something private and because of that most people or even angels don't go around boasting of their sexual relationships. Most of us tend to be quiet about that side of our lives and for good reason. It is generally nobody else's business! In the physical life marriage can provide a safe environment for the children.

C.34 RELATIONSHIPS IN THE SPIRIT WORLD. As in regard to relationships in heaven. I can tell you that they are much more beautiful and a more complete experience than in the physical or temporal world.

Much is hidden from us now .. as heaven is by definition a reward after this very difficult physical life. A physical temporal world that unfortunately has been usurped by Satan a very long time ago - 6000 years ago. Our present life on earth is filled with struggle against evil, sickness, pain, sorrow, frustration and disappointment. That is to say apart from all the wonderful things that also happen to people.

C.35 GETTING SAVED:

It is so important to receive Jesus as our Saviour so that we can all go to heaven after this temporal physical life that will soon be past.

C.36 THE AGE OF A MAN?

Imagine King David mentioned that 'A man's life shall be 70 or '3 score' and ten years. We don't get much time on this planet at present! Best to use one's time wisely!

C.37 I am myself already 72, which in modern times is considered to be a 'younger' old person. Unfortunately, Satan and his cohorts have been very busy polluting the planet in modern times with all kinds of poisons which are reducing the lifespan of mankind as we speak. I heard recently that the C and V from 2020 have reduced man's lifespan from 78 to 73! Wow! Such a poisoning of the planet. That is why I say avoid the V at all costs.

C.38 This physical life is not the time and place where one gets to see all of your dreams fulfilled and where all is bliss - at least not if you are doing God's will. This life was intended by God Himself to be a struggle.

We must fight against the evil and the demonic and against Satan himself.

It has been like that since the Garden of Eden.

(Please read my book *Eden Insights*) to see the great struggle that it was for the very first man and woman on this planet! Satan was really pestering them and trying to kill them all the time! Satan does it on a world scale using his insane Globalists and their cohorts.

SPIRITUAL FIGHT

C.39 We have seen the 'Riding forth of the 4 Horseman of Revelation 6 fame. –

1) White Horse of Government

2) Red Horse of War

3) Black Horse of the Merchants of Wealth

4) Pale horse of Death & Hell.

It has never been on such a scale as since the modern age from around 1910 onwards. Each one of us is having to face all kinds of spiritual battles, emotional battles, physical battles including financial troubles.

C.40 Many of us face sorrows of having lost a love one to Death itself like myself having lost our lively and beautiful 34-year-old daughter to terminal cancer last year in August 2024. At least we know where she went because we believe in God and heaven.

C.41 No. this life is anything but easy. The Key is to be positive and to fully realize that according to the scriptures there is indeed coming a much better world where all of your dreams do indeed come true. It is very important to fully realise that if you are a godly person, then you will probably have a hard time one way of the other in this physical life.

C.42 What I like to do is protest against the Evil and expose Satan and his endless lies. I also like to bring out the truth in as many ways as possible as the organized religions seem to be mostly sleeping in Satan's make-believe world.

Ephesians 6.12 "For we wrestle not against flesh and blood, but against principalities, against powers, against the rulers of the darkness of this world, against spiritual wickedness in high *places*."

C.43 I know that a much better world is awaiting all of us who believe in Jesus as He Himself told us.

John 14 'Behold I go to prepare a place for you that where I am there ye shall be also. Yes, Jesus has prepared for us the Holy City of New Jerusalem – See also *Revelation 21-22*

CHAPTER 16: ENDTIMES: LAST 7 YEARS OF HISTORY? *Has it already begun in 2025?*

What has the Holy Spirit Mother got to do with the LAST DAYS AND THE ENDTIME? If you look at the picture on the front cover of this book you will see her embracing the world as her desire is to bring peace and love to the world. Unfortunately, many negative End-time events have to happen first according to the Bible before the Golden Age of the Millennium or the Age of Peace.

C.1 Our planet is quickly descending into the greatest darkness in history. That is unbelief in God and total disobedience to His commands. Every day we hear of wars and rumours of wars even threats of nuclear war. We are told that many catastrophes are about to happen. Where is the long-foretold **Antichrist?** Is he perhaps already pulling the strings? What about **666** as foretold in the Book of Revelation? In these modern times it is exactly as Jesus warned in *Matthew 24*. It would appear that all the things mentioned in the *Book of Revelation* are about to unfold. May God help us all. We would seem to be close to the *End of the World* as being in the *Last Days*. What do the scriptures say about these present times?

THE LAST DAYS

2 Timothy 3.1-4

[1] This know also, that in the last days perilous times shall come.

[2] For men shall be lovers of their own selves, covetous, boasters, proud, blasphemers, ...

[3] Without natural affection, trucebreakers, false accusers, incontinent, fierce, despisers of ...

[4] Traitors, heady, high-minded, lovers of pleasures more than lovers of God;

SIGNS OF THE TIMES

MATTHEW 24.3-8,15

[3] And as he sat upon the mount of Olives, the disciples came unto him privately, saying, Tell us, when shall these things be? and what shall be the sign of thy coming, and of the end of the world?

[4] And Jesus answered and said unto them, Take heed that no man deceive you.

[5] For many shall come in my name, saying, I am Christ; and shall deceive many.

[6] And ye shall hear of wars and rumours of wars: see that ye be not troubled: for all these things must come to pass, but the end is not yet.

[7] For nation shall rise against nation, and kingdom against kingdom: and there shall be famines, and pestilences, and earthquakes, in divers places.

⁸ All these are the beginning of sorrows.

¹²And because iniquity shall abound, the love of many shall wax cold.

¹³But he that shall endure unto the end, the same shall be saved.

¹⁴And this gospel of the kingdom shall be preached in all the world for a witness unto all nations; and then shall the end come.

1 John 2.18 "Little children, it is the last time: and as ye have heard that antichrist shall come, even now are there many antichrists; whereby we know that it is the last time."

Abomination of Desolation = The Mark of The Beast 666 = Digital I.D. 666 Implants

Matthew 24.15

15 When ye therefore shall see the abomination of desolation, spoken of by Daniel the prophet, stand in the holy place.

C.2 This verse is clearly talking about the 3rd Temple in Jerusalem being built and the Antichrist comes along and sets up his '*666 Mark of the Beast*' based in Jerusalem in the new 3rd Temple, soon to be built. Apparently, they already have the pre-fab 3rd temple job read.

ECONOMIC CRASH

1 Thessalonians 5.3

³ For when they shall say, 'Peace and safety'; then sudden destruction cometh upon them, as travail upon a woman with child; and they shall not escape.

C.3 Will we soon see the 3rd Temple in Jerusalem built as prophesied 2000 years ago? Will the Antichrist indeed arise in 2025? When will the 7-Year Covenant of the infamous Antichrist start? What about the Great Tribulation of 3 and a half years and the Rapture?

C.4 What will '*they*' engineer to happen next to bring on the 3rd Temple and the Rise of the Antichrist? Probably some big disaster including a total meltdown of the world's economic system Definition: 'They' = The Controllers =Globalists.

THE ANTICHRIST

1 John 2.18 "Little children, it is the last time: and as ye have heard that antichrist shall come, even now are there many antichrists; whereby we know that it is the last time."

Daniel 8.23-25

²³ And in the latter time of their kingdom, when the transgressors are come to the full, a king of fierce countenance, and understanding dark sentences, shall stand up.

²⁴ And his power shall be mighty, but not by his own power: and he shall destroy

wonderfully, and shall prosper, and practise, and shall destroy the mighty and the holy people.

[25] And through his policy also he shall cause craft to prosper in his hand; and he shall magnify himself in his heart, and by peace shall destroy many: he shall also stand up against the Prince of princes; but he shall be broken without hand.

2 Thessalonians 2.3-4

[3] Let no man deceive you by any means: for that day shall not come, except there comes a falling away first, and that man of sin be revealed, the son of perdition;

[4] Who opposes and exalts himself above all that is called God, or that is worshipped; so that he as God sits in the temple of God, shewing himself that he is God.

THE GREAT TRIBULATION

Matthew 24.21-22,29-31

[21] For then shall be *great tribulation*, such as was not since the beginning of the world to this time, no, nor ever shall be.

[22] And except those days should be shortened, there should no flesh be saved: but for the elect's sake those days shall be shortened.

REVELATION CHAPTER 8.7-13

[7] The first angel sounded, and there followed hail and fire mingled with blood, and they were cast upon the earth: and the third part of trees was burnt up, and all green grass was burnt up.

[8] And the second angel sounded, and as it were a great mountain burning with fire was cast into the sea: and the third part of the sea became blood;

[9] And the third part of the creatures which were in the sea, and had life, died; and the third part of the ships were destroyed.

[10] And the third angel sounded, and there fell a great star from heaven, burning as it were a lamp, and it fell upon the third part of the rivers, and upon the fountains of waters;

[11] And the name of the star is called Wormwood: and the third part of the waters became wormwood; and many men died of the waters, because they were made bitter.

[12] And the fourth angel sounded, and the third part of the sun was smitten, and the third part of the moon, and the third part of the stars; so as the third part of them was darkened, and the day shone not for a third part of it, and the night likewise.

[13] And I beheld, and heard an angel flying through the midst of heaven, saying with a loud voice, Woe, woe, woe, to the inhabitants of the earth by reason of the other voices of the trumpet of the three angels, which are yet to sound!

C.5 Yes, we are all longing for the 2nd Coming of Jesus Christ. I honestly think that indeed time is running out and soon according to the scripture 'Time shall be no more'.

Revelation 10:6 "And sware by Him that lives for ever and ever, Who created heaven, and the things that therein are, and the earth, and the things therein, and the sea, and the things which are therein, that there should be *TIME NO LONGER*:"

C.6 Lets all keep our eyes on heaven and the coming Marriage Supper of the Lamb.

REVELATION 19:9 And he saith unto me, Write, Blessed are they which are called unto the *marriage supper of the Lamb*...." "And he saith unto me, Write, Blessed are they which are called unto the marriage supper of the Lamb. And he saith unto me, These are the true sayings of God."

THE RAPTURE

1 THESSALONIANS 4.13-17

[13] But I would not have you to be ignorant, brethren, concerning them which are asleep (dead in Christ), that ye sorrow not, even as others which have no hope.

[14] For if we believe that Jesus died and rose again, even so them also which sleep in Jesus will God bring with him.

[15] For this we say unto you by the word of the Lord, that we which are alive and remain unto the coming of the *Lord* shall not prevent them which are asleep.

[16 For] the **Lord** himself shall descend from heaven with a shout, with the voice of the archangel, and with the trump of God: and the dead in Christ shall rise first:

[17] Then we which are alive and remain shall be caught up together with them in the clouds, to meet the Lord in the air: and so shall we ever be with the Lord.

1 Corinthians 15.51-52

[51] Behold, I shew you a mystery; We shall not all sleep, but we shall all be changed,

[52] In a moment, in the twinkling of an eye, at the last trump: for the trumpet shall sound, and the dead shall be raised incorruptible, and we shall be changed.

THE 2ND COMING OF CHRIST

[29] Immediately *after the tribulation* of those days shall the sun be darkened, and the moon shall not give her light, and the stars shall fall from heaven, and the powers of the heavens shall be shaken:

[30] And *then* shall *appear the sign of the Son of man in heaven*: and then shall all the tribes of the earth mourn, and they shall see the Son of man coming in the clouds of heaven with power and great glory.

[31] And he shall send his angels with a great sound of a trumpet, and they shall *gather*

together his elect from the four winds, from one end of heaven to the other.

MARRIAGE SUPPER OF THE LAMB

Revelation 19.7-9

[7] Let us be glad and rejoice and give honour to him: for the marriage of the Lamb is come, and his wife hath made herself ready.

[8] And to her was granted that she should be arrayed in fine linen, clean and white: for the fine linen is the righteousness of saints.

[9] And he saith unto me, Write, Blessed are they which are called unto the marriage supper of the Lamb. And he saith unto me, these are the true sayings of God.

2 Corinthians 5.10

"For we must all appear before the judgment seat of Christ; that everyone may receive the things *done* in *his* body, according to that he hath done, whether *it be* good or bad."

Daniel 12.2-3

[2-3] And many of them that sleep in the dust of the earth shall awake, some to everlasting life, and some to shame and everlasting contempt. 3 And they that be wise shall shine as the brightness of the firmament; and they that turn many to righteousness as the stars for ever and ever.

CHAPTER 17: A CHRISTMAS STORY - 'MOTHER CHRISTMAS'

C.1 What The Bible Says About The Holy Spirit Mother My Audio On Youtube: 'CHRISTMAS MOTHER': HAPPY CHRISTMAS EVERYONE! www.youtube.com/watch?v=_UF147OfFyA&t=209s

Many things in the Bible make a lot more sense when one realises that we have God the Father and God the Mother and God the Son.

C.2 Look at the story of Mary and the birth of Jesus her Son in the Gospel of Luke.

Luke 1.6-29 And in the sixth month the angel Gabriel was sent from God unto a city of Galilee, named Nazareth, to a virgin espoused to a man whose name was Joseph, of the house of David; and the virgin's name was Mary. And the angel came in unto her, and said, Hail, thou that art highly favoured, the Lord is with thee: blessed art thou among women. And when she saw him, she was troubled at his saying and cast in her mind what manner of salutation this should be.

[30] And the angel said unto her, Fear not, Mary: for thou hast found favour with God. And, behold, thou shalt conceive in thy womb, and bring forth a son, and shalt call his name Jesus. He shall be great, and shall be called the Son of the Highest: and the Lord God shall give unto him the throne of his father David: And he shall reign over the house of Jacob for ever; and of his kingdom there shall be no end.

[34] Then said Mary unto the angel, how shall this be, seeing I know not a man? And the angel answered and said unto her, The Holy Ghost shall come upon thee, and the power of the Highest shall overshadow thee: therefore, also that holy thing which shall be born of thee shall be called the Son of God.

Mary is visited by the archangel Gabriel who tells her that she is 'highly favoured, the Lord is with thee: blessed art thou among women.

C.3 Why does the angel say this? Because Mary is destined to become the mother of the Saviour Jesus Christ. She is told that she will conceive in her womb and bring forth the Messiah that has been promised to the Jewish nation for thousands of years.

Mary is amazed by this statement and says to the angel Gabriel 'How shall this be, seeing I know not a man?

Notice the full reality of what Gabriel the archangel tells Mary.

[35] And the angel answered and said unto her, The Holy Ghost (Mother) shall come upon thee, and the *power of the Highest* shall overshadow thee: therefore, also that holy thing which shall be born of thee shall be called the Son of God.

C.4 When we know that there is the Holy Spirit Mother in the Trinity then how did her Son Jesus get born on earth? This verse of Luke 1.35 explains it very well. '*The Holy Ghost* shall come upon thee, and the *power of the Highest* shall *overshadow thee*:

C.5 This above verse would indicate that the Holy Spirit Mother would come into Mary and that she would be joined by her husband Father God and that Jesus would be conceived in the physical body of Mary. The above verse Luke 1.35 makes it crystal clear that for Mary to get pregnant and have baby Jesus that it going to take both the Holy Spirit Mother and God the Father. Of course, it takes both a man and a woman to make a baby both in the physical dimension as well as the spiritual dimension.

C.6 Many people from the churches have been falsely indoctrinated into the idea that there is 'no marriage in heaven' or no male and female of male female relationships such as marriage - no sex in heaven. Nothing could be further from the truth. Those of the churches constantly misquote scriptures from the Bible often not knowing the original intent of the example given in the Bible. Most of the church people don't even study their Bibles but just quote the hearsay doctrines of their churches.

C.7 The verse mentioned concerning marriage is a verse spoken by Jesus. Let's examine this verse in detail.

Matthew 22.30 For in the resurrection they neither marry, nor are given in marriage, but are as the angels of God in heaven.

Let's examine the context where Jesus said this exact verse.

In this chapter of Matthew 22 Jesus was describing the Kingdom of Heaven and explaining that it was a very different place than the physical realm at least in some ways.

In Matthew 22.29-32 Jesus answered and said unto them, Ye do err, not knowing the scriptures, nor the power of God. For in the resurrection, they neither marry, nor are given in marriage, but are as the angels of God in heaven. But as touching the resurrection of the dead, have ye not read that which was spoken unto you by God, saying, I am the God of Abraham, and the God of Isaac, and the God of Jacob? God is not the God of the dead, but of the living.

C.8 First of all, let's examine the angels of God. Are they *only male* as many claim, or are there also female angels? All we need to do is look to the Bible to Genesis 6 to find out that there were masculine angels of God having intercourse with the women on the earth. What does that tell us? It is telling us plainly that there must be female angels by deduction.

C.9 Some people have asked me well why didn't the fallen angels stay with the female angels in heaven? Now that is a very good question. The simple answer is because the Fallen angels were in rebellion against God and they would not get on with the female angels in heaven. When the Fallen angels rebelled and fell to the physical earth and started to have intercourse with the human women it was more out a form of escapism from the spirit world and from the direct presence of God and His Holy Spirit Mother and Jesus their Son. As time went by the Fallen angels became more and more obsessed with destroying God's Creation and they became more and more perverse.

C.10 1stly: Jesus stating 'For in the resurrection they neither marry, nor are given in marriage, but are as the angels of God in heaven' does not mean that there is no male and female in heaven. It also does not mean that people don't have sex in heaven. Jesus was just stating that relationships are not bound by earthly marriage vows that we have on planet earth. He was answering a silly question by the Sadducees who asked Him about the Resurrection, when they themselves didn't believe in the resurrection - one of their 'made up stories' about a woman who had supposedly been married 7 times to 7 brothers one after the other when each one of them had died. So, Jesus gave them an abrupt answer without expounding upon it as they would not believe anyway.

C.11 2ndly: Jesus stating 'For in the resurrection they neither marry, nor are given in marriage, but are as the angels of God in heaven' does not mean that there is no male and female in heaven. It also does not mean that people don't have sex in heaven. Of course they do, otherwise the Creation of peoples could not continue. We all need to understand how important God's original command to Adam and Eve was. It was also the same exact command that God gave to Noah and his sons after the Great Flood 'Be fruitful and multiply'

Genesis 1.26-28 And God said, 'Let us make man in our image, after our likeness: and let them have dominion over the fish of the sea, and over the fowl of the air, and over the cattle, and over all the earth, and over every creeping thing that creeps upon the earth.'

C.12 Notice God stated our image as God the Father was talking to His wife the Holy Spirit Mother.

[27] So God created man in his own image, in the image of God created he him; male and female created he them.

God made them both male and female in the image of God the Father (male) and in the image of the Holy Spirit Mother. (female)

[28] And God blessed them, and God said unto them, 'Be fruitful, and multiply', and replenish the earth, and subdue it: and have dominion over the fish of the sea, and over the fowl of the air, and over every living thing that moves upon the earth.

CHAPTER 18: Will There Be Marriage in Heaven?

C.1 The following is what is stated by the churches in general:

'Marriage in Heaven will be on a much higher plane because the church will be united with Christ.'

Example No1) Marriage is the first institution God gave on Earth, and it is a wonderful relationship. He provided this special union to alleviate loneliness (Genesis 2:18) and for the purpose of populating the Earth (Genesis 9:7). In Heaven, there will be no loneliness—fellowship will be more than the human mind can understand, and Heaven will be populated by the saints born of God. 'While we cannot fathom not knowing our spouses or children in the earthly sense, Jesus tells us not to worry about these things. *"A time is coming when I will no longer use this kind of language. ... I have told you these things, so that in me you may have peace. ... Take heart! I have overcome the world"* (John 16:25, 33). Marriage as we know it in its human form will not be practiced in Heaven because it will be perfected in the Lord **Jesus Christ.** Although our human minds cannot fully understand heavenly things, the day is coming when we will comprehend all great truths—including this one. - Billy Graham

Example No 2 Here is another opinion: 'Jesus does not address *why* people will not marry at the resurrection. Some have speculated that marriage won't exist in the resurrected state because procreation will not be necessary. Some suggest that marriage, as a symbol of Christ and His people (Ephesians 5:22–23), will not be necessary as the reality will have replaced the symbol. Either way, Jesus is making several things clear: 1) there is certainly a resurrection; 2) this state of being will be drastically different from what humanity experiences now; 3) marriage will not occur; and 4) humanity will be like the angels, who also do not marry.' - Why will people neither marry nor be given in marriage in the resurrection (Matthew 22:30)? | GotQuestions.org

MARRIAGE IN HEAVEN?

C.2 It is amazing how messed up the so-called Christian churches are as to what they teach, as much of it is not actually in the scriptures, and they have misinterpreted what the original scriptures have said in ancient Hebrew.

They always state *'Matthew 22:30* states, angels "neither marry nor are given in marriage." - so no sex in heaven. That however is not what Jesus stated.

C.3 The truth be said, 'Male and Female are the whole basis of God's original Creation' starting with the Holy Spirit Mother being Mother God and Mother of all Creation along with God the Father of Creation. There has always been male and female both in the spirit world and in the physical world which is but a temporal reflection of the much greater spirit world.

C.4 Without male and female there would not be any babies and children. The difference between male and female brings a lot of Joy to God's creations as well as the babies that are born to them.

C.5 Of course, I can understand that God has hidden from the eyes of most people how things really are in the spirit world, because most people can't be trusted with the truth in many cases.

C.6 Knowing 'too much' in Pre-Flood times caused chaos as mankind were led astray by angels who fell and took the daughters of Cain as their wives upon the earth. This also showed that angels do have sex.

C.7 The churches are in general so messed up about sex when it was God that created sex, and it was not sex that caused the original Fall of Man as preached by some of the churches.

C.8 In some ways I can understand that point of view, because as I have already pointed out in my other Insights books that Cain was fathered by Satan in the Garden of Eden. We also know that some 500 years after the Creation the Fallen angels came down and had sex with the licentious Luciferian daughters of Cain who were into all kinds of sexual mischief. However, the fall of mankind was sin not sex. Disobedience to God's commandments.

C.9 Ever since Satan screwed up in the Garden of Eden he has been trying to destroy normal sex, marriage, Men and women, babies and children as he seeks to destroy all that God has created.

Satan is a total reprobate and not one to be trusted.

One day after Jesus has returned to the earth in the 2nd Coming of Christ, the true balance of nature will be restored.

That includes the balance between male and female and marriage and the having babies and families as God originally taught mankind.

People will be much happier in a properly balanced world where there is no perversion of the rich and so-called elite, or the merchants of the earth as mentioned in the Book of Revelations chapters 17-18.

C.10 REALITY OF SEX, MARRIAGE AND FAMILES

Male and Female are the whole basis of God's original Creation starting with the Holy Spirit Mother being Mother God and Mother of all Creation along with God the Father of Creation.

[See my book *'Secrets of Enoch Insights'*, to know more about the Holy Spirit Mother also known as Wisdom and the Divine Feminine. You will read about Pravuil who is yet another name for the Holy Spirit or Wisdom (Wisdom = Sophia in Greek.]

C.11 MARRIAGE IN HEAVEN: **In conclusion**: The problem is that the organized religions are often really lost when it comes to talking about sensitive things like sex. I am much more liberal in my thinking and would imagine that anything that God has created as very pleasurable would not be totally abandoned in the world to come, but rather improved and glorified without the physical limitations – no longer messy as stated in a famous movie. Of course, marriage is a lot more than physical intimacy and is about loving companionship and caring for another.

C.12 One thing for sure is that dying and going home to be with Jesus will be total ecstasy. I can hardly wait to go home to heaven. My idea of heaven is that you will be wonderfully united with all those that you have loved in this physical life and that you will have a much clearer understanding of each person that God brought into your life as witnessed by those who have testified of 'Life After Death Experiences'. We will be reunited with all our loved ones that have died. I think love is going to expand in your personal experience, as you enter the spirit world of Love and Joy and peace, praise, thankfulness, understanding, total fulfilment, reward, as well as sheer ecstasy.

C.13 LACK OF MARRIAGES AND CHILDREN TODAY: Sadly, in modern times in the Western world, so many people have turned against both marriage and in having children to the point that we no longer have the 2.1 children/couple needed to replenish the human race but only 1.2 children/couple average. Also, tragically 54% of women don't get married until after the age of 30 which according to experts is not a good idea. In studying gynaecology, we find that the woman's body is best suited with having children at the age of 22-25 for her first child. Sadly, I just yesterday read about the fact that 54% of women are not married by the age of '40' years old these days in the Western world. Of those 40 years and under 28% of men think that marriage is important and only 18% of woman do. Bye-bye to a future Western world! What has happened here in the West? The West will soon be on extinction level. What has happened to people's sex drive? Has it been deliberately destroyed by too many chemicals? It is true that we have all heard of the severe reduction in fertility in both the mane and women since Covid and the hellish vaccines.

C.14 It is also tragic that in today's world we now have 73,000,000 abortions each year. I believe that someone has to take care of all of the spirits of those babies that are aborted in this life. So, there must be many loving mothers in heaven to make up for the cruelty these babies faced on the earth. Did you know that there are more babies aborted each year than the total number of people (non-babies) who die each year = 60,000,000.

C.15 I just saw the newspapers boasting how that everyone is single these days. I also read how so many old coupes are divorcing and people abandoning their spouses. The spirit of 'caring and loving' is being pushed aside in modern times as this world tries to make people into soulless robotic automatons to work in this make-believe Matrix world of 'dog eat dog'.

Our relationships on earth.

C.16 On earth we are very limited in our relationships with other people for many reasons. One of the problems with the temporal life is lack of time. In the spirit world there is no time, which would greatly facilitate having a much greater understanding of each person and their situation without always being under pressure of time.

LIFE AFTER DEATH

C.17 I will give you a typical example. In the Life After Death Experiences, one will typically hear a patient mention that when they first died that they found themselves hovering above their bodies and they descried the frantic attempts of doctors to resuscitate their bodies, whilst their spirits were well and unperturbed even though they themselves had just died. They felt free from the weight of the flesh and the old body. When they were in this state of the spirit world, they became more and more relaxed about everything, and they were not worried by the fact that they were now dead. As a spirit helper took them by the hand and led them away to heaven, they noticed that they could understand what all the people in the room were thinking.

ADVANTAGE OF THE SPIRIT WORLD

C.18 If time is not an issue, then it would be much easier to plan things. It would also be a place to fully understand other people. In the physical life most of us feel separated from most of the other people in the world most of the time. Imagine being in a different world of the spirit where you can perfectly understand each other. I think that we will feel like children in the presence of God the Father and His precious Holy Spirit Mother and Jesus their Son. Imagine being in a place where God is acknowledged, and everyone behaves in a godly manner. No cross bosses or bossy people. A place where all have learned to restrain their spirits and only 'speak' when necessary. A beautiful place where we are forgiven for the wrong things that we did on earth and God does not hold anything against us. A place where I think most of us will be learning new things all the time. We will experience God to the full and more fully understand Him our Creator and to understand exactly the purpose of everything. The most precious experience will be to see our Saviour Jesus and our Husband in the spirit as we more fully realize that we collectively are the Bride of Christ and not just little children.

THE TEMPORAL LIFE ON EARTH

C.19 The physical stage of our lives on earth had a very good purpose. 1) Being a baby 2) Being a small child 3) Being an older child 4) being a teenager 5) Being a young adult 6) Being an adult 7) Being middle-aged 8) an older person 9) Aged

Each of these different phases is of great importance to God.

When one is a baby, it gives a great opportunity for God and the Holy Spirit to show much love to that new soul - mostly through human beings about them. If great love is shown to this small child, it will grow up being a loving person. Once it is of age, this soul must make its own decisions in life as to how it is going to behave towards both God and others. I can tell you from a life of experience with myself now being older at 72 that it is God's Word that has kept me all my life. By that I mean that I read God's Word every day to keep me inspired and closer to heaven and the spiritual realm -especially in a world that is full of darkness and ungodliness, and unbelief is rampant. I look forward to going home to heaven in the not-too-distant future as I know that everything will be perfected there with Jesus and His precious Holy Spirit Mother with Salvation.

CHAPTER 19: BIBLE MENTIONS OF HOLY SPIRIT

C.1 Here are just a few verses from the KJV of the Bible mentioning the Spirit of God, which is really talking about Holy Spirit Mother and her caring for us as her children as well as protecting us and instructing us in the ways of the Lord.:

NB All the old Hebrew books mention the Spirit of God and denote her as being a feminine being. She is known as Ruach, the Spirit of God and Wisdom as in the Proverbs of Solomon. Widom of Solomon, Ecclesiasticus and many other ancient Hebrew Apocryphal books.

Romans 8.16 The Spirit itself bears witness with our spirit, that we are the children of God:

C.2 You can see in this verse that the Holy Spirit is in close communion with us her children.

1 Corinthians 2.10 But God hath revealed them unto us by his *Spirit*: for the *Spirit* searches all things, yea, the deep things of God.

C.3 Holy Spirit Mother goes out of her way to find Gods position on any given topic and she shows it to us, her children.

1 John 4.2 Hereby know ye the *Spirit of God*: Every spirit that confesses that Jesus Christ is come in the flesh is of God:

C.4 There are those who claim to be Christians but they have not the Spirit of God which is a loving and caring Spirit not hateful, negative, accusing condemning others Not perfectionists- as many religionists are.

Romans 8.9 But ye are not in the flesh, but in the *Spirit*, if so be that the Spirit of God dwell in you. Now if any man have not the *Spirit* of Christ, he is none of his.

Psalm 119.96 I have seen an end of all perfection: but thy commandment is exceeding broad.

C.5 It is important to receive Jesus as our Saviour into our hearts and to also ask for the anointing of the Holy Spirit who will give us the power and anointing to be a witness for God -to give us enough love to sacrifice our owns lives in order to live for Christ as one of His disciples preaching the gospel of Salvation.

1 Corinthians 2.2 Now we have received, not the spirit of the world, but the *spirit* which is of God; that we might know the things that are freely given to us of God.

C.6 The secret is that you have to have the Spirit of God in order to know the truth in full as it is given from heaven.

1 John 4.6 We are of God: he that knows God heareth us; he that is not of God heareth not us. Hereby know we the *spirit* of truth, and the spirit of error.

C.7 This is an accurate statement just by observation. Some people will listen to our witness of Salvation through the Messiah Jesus Christ and yet others refuse to want to know.

Ezekial 11.24 Afterwards the spirit took me up, and brought me in a vision by the *Spirit of God* into Chaldea, to them of the captivity. So, the vision that I had seen went up from me.

C.8 It is indeed Spirit of God who takes us up to see visions or dream dreams of heaven.

1 Corinthians 2.11 For what man knows the things of a man, save the spirit of man which is in him? Even so the things of God knows no man, but the *Spirit of God.*

C.9 It is so important to be praying about everything we do and thus be led by the Spirit of God. She can tell us things about a situation before it even happens. Afterall, there is no time in the spirit world.

John 4.24 God is a Spirit: and they that worship him must worship him in spirit and in truth.

C.10 What is this saying? If we want to worship God then we do it through the *Truth*. Jesus is the truth according to John 14.6.

John 14.6 'I am the way the truth and life, no man cometh unto the Father but be Me. Neither is there salvation in any other. For there is no other name under heaven given among men whereby we must be saved.

C.11 The Spirit of God points to the way of Salvation and She is both loving and tender-hearted.

Isaiah 11.2 And the *spirit of the LORD*, shall rest upon Him (The Messiah) , the spirit of wisdom and understanding, the spirit of counsel and might, the spirit of knowledge and of the fear of the LORD;

C.12 This verse clearly shows that the Holy Spirit Mother is taking care of her Son the Messiah.

John 3.34 For he whom God hath sent speak the words of God: for God giveth not the *Spirit* by measure unto him.

C.13 When you have the Spirit of God there is 'no limit' to what might be given to you by the Spirit of God. Think of how much was given to Moses and all that was given to Jesus.

Matthew 12.28 But if I cast out devils by the *Spirit of God,* then the kingdom of God is come unto you.

C.14 Amazing how that evil spirits in people can be cast out through God's Holy Spirit. This also applies to haunted or disturbed buildings.

Ezekiel 1.20 Whithersoever the *spirit* was to go, they went, thither was their spirit to go; and the wheels were lifted up over against them: for the spirit of the living creature was in the wheels.

C.15 The Spirit of God was in the wheels. For the spirit of the living creatures was in the wheels. How can wheels be alive being at least seemingly mechanical but not physical of course.? Very strange description. I suppose this description is very strange for us humans as it would seem that an earthly comparison would be if a mechanical device on earth like a car was *alive* like the Herbie-car in the old movie.

1 Corinthians 6.20 For ye are bought with a price: therefore glorify God in your body, and in your spirit, which are God's.

C.16 Jesus is the One who paid the price for our Salvation and therefore we owe it to God to behave ourselves in a godly manner.

1 Corinthians 3.16 Know ye not that ye are the temple of God, and that the *Spirit of God* dwelleth in you?

C.17 A temple is a building, that when empty, is able to contain others things like people. God wants us to invite the Spirit of God to dwell in us. If Holy Spirit Mother lives within us then we need to make our building acceptable for her and inviting through our humility and love towards Jesus.

Psalm 51.10 Create in me a clean heart, O God; and renew a right spirit within me.

C.18 Cause me to have a humble and contrite heart, O God; renew my spirit by your Holy Spirit.

Romans 8.14 For as many as are led by the *Spirit of God*, they are the sons of God.

C.19 Led by Holy Spirit Mother as we are her sons and desire to please her our Mother.

Hebrews 9.14 How much more shall the blood of Christ, who through the *eternal Spirit* offered himself without spot to God, purge your conscience from dead works to serve the living God?

C.20 This shows that Jesus worked very much together with His Mother - Holy Spirit Mother to gave his life as a sacrifice to God for the sins of the world.

Galatians 5.25 If we live in the *Spirit*, let us also walk in the *Spirit*.

C.21 If we have the Holy Ghost or Holy Spirit then we should use her power in order to be a witness for Jesus and His love and Salvation.

Ephesians 2.22 In whom ye also are built together for an habitation of God through the *Spirit*.

C.22 The Holy Spirit Mother is the One who builds the true church of God through all the members. Who having a form of godliness but denying the power thereof.

2 Tim 3.5,7 Having a form of godliness but denying the power thereof: from such turn away., Ever learning, and never able to come to the knowledge of the truth.

C.23 Most of the religious people of the world have a 'form of godliness' but they deny the power of the Holy Ghost, as the scripture states:' Ever learning and never coming to the knowledge of the truth. Jesus stated, 'I am the Way the Truth and the Life, no man cometh unto the Father but by Me'. We cannot come to God without Jesus the Saviour and that is the mistake that most religions make.

C.24 Here are some Bible verses on the Holy Ghost which is the same as the Holy Spirit: We could call them Holy Ghost Mother as well as Holy Spirit Mother or Wisdom = Sophia (Greek) The true feminine representative of God.

John 14.26 But the Comforter, which is the Holy Ghost, whom the Father will send in my name, She (not He) shall teach you all things, and bring all things to your remembrance, whatsoever I have said unto you.

C.25 The Comforter acts like a Mother because She is a Mother. Like a mother she comforts her children and teaches them the ways of righteousness as taught by Jesus Christ the Messiah - Her Son.

Acts 2.38 Then Peter said unto them, Repent, and be baptized every one of you in the name of Jesus Christ for the remission of sins, and ye shall receive the gift of the *Holy Ghost*.

C.26 'Repent and be baptized' in essence means 'rent your heart' and not your garment and cry out to God for the forgiveness of all of your sins. Getting baptized is not a religious ceremony but simply asking Jesus into your heart that you might be saved eternally. Receiving the Holy Ghost is normally a separate action from getting saved and She the Holy Spirit Mother is for the anointing to empower a person to witness about Christ being the Saviour. Also to empower one to pray for others to also receive Jesus into their hearts as their Saviour. - John 3.36 He that believe on the Son has eternal life.

John 1.32-34 And John bare record, saying, I saw the *Spirit* descending from heaven like a dove, and it abode upon him. And I knew him not: but he that sent me to baptize with water, the same said unto me, Upon whom thou shalt see the *Spirit* descending, and remaining on him, the same is he which baptizes with the *Holy Ghost*. And I saw, and bare record that this is the Son of God.

C.27 Here we see Jesus Baptising through Holy Ghost His Mother as She brings rebirth to souls.

Titus 3.5 Not by works of righteousness which we have done, but according to his mercy he saved us, by the washing of regeneration, and renewing of the *Holy Ghost*.

C.28 How does the baptism of the *Holy Spirit* renew us. The difference between getting saved and getting the anointing of the *Holy Spirit*. Many people pray to receive Jesus but fail to get the anointing of the *Holy Spirit* who empowers God's children to witness and tell others about Jesus and Salvation. However, the *Spirit* of God is not given to everyone but unto those who obey God and do what Jesus commanded to 'Go into all the world and preach the Gospel of Salvation through Jesus Christ unto every creature.'.

Acts 5.32 And we are his witnesses of these things; and so is also the *Holy Ghost*, whom God hath given to them that obey Him.

C.29 If we want to have the full power of the *Holy Ghost* then we need to obey what God is telling us to do at any given moment. God tries to send us messages by His *Holy Spirit* but it all depends on if we listen to them and follow through on those messages.

Acts 1.8 But ye shall receive power, after that the *Holy Ghost* is come upon you: and ye shall be witnesses unto me both in Jerusalem, and in all Judaea, and in Samaria, and unto the uttermost part of the earth.

C.30 We receive the power to tell others about Jesus by praying with them to receive the Lord Jesus into their hearts and to be filled with His *Holy Spirit*. The *Holy Spirit Mother* gives God's disciples the power and anointing to be bold and stand up for Jesus.

Romans 8.26-27 Likewise the Spirit also helps our infirmities: for we know not what we should pray for as we ought: but the Spirit itself maketh intercession for us with groanings which cannot be uttered.

C.31 Speaking in tongues which cannot be uttered -the language of heaven which few understand, but God does.

John 16.13 Howbeit when She, the *Spirit of truth*, is come, She will guide you into all truth: for She shall not speak of herself; but whatsoever She shall hear, that shall She speak: and She will shew you things to come.

C.32 Notice that I have put *She* instead of the traditional he, as *She* was the original in Hebrew language.

Ephesians 4.30 And grieve not the *Holy Spirit* of God, whereby ye are sealed unto the day of redemption.

C.33 Jesus warned us not to grieve the Spirit of God as that would not be forgiven in this world or the next.

John 8.32 And ye shall know the truth, and the truth shall make you free.

C.34 When you know Jesus in person as well as the truth about His *Holy Spirit Mother* it sets you free from all of Satan's lies.

John 3.5 Jesus answered, Verily, verily, I say unto thee, Except a man be born of water and of the *Spirit*, he cannot enter into the kingdom of God.

C.35 The *Holy Spirit Mother* being female is the one who gives birth to all the souls that get saved just like a physical baby in the womb of water a spiritual baby is born by the *Holy Spirit Mother*. I know that it is difficult to understand spiritual things when you can't see them but we can see the effects.

1 Corinthians 3.16-17 Know ye not that ye are the temple of God, and that the *Spirit of God* dwelleth in you?

C.36 We are the temple of God when *God's Spirit* abides in us.

Romans 15.13 Now the God of hope fill you with all joy and peace in believing, that ye may abound in hope, through the power of the *Holy Ghost*.

C.37 The *Holy Ghost* being the same as the *Holy Spirit* fills us with joy and peace because of our faith in Jesus Her Son, as we believe in simple salvation by grace.

Luke 1.35 And the angel answered and said unto her, The *Holy Ghost* shall come upon thee, and the power of the Highest shall overshadow thee: therefore also that holy thing which shall be born of thee shall be called the Son of God.

C.38 This is an amazing verse which is clearly showing the involvement of both God the Father and the *Holy Spirit Mother* in order to create their Son Jesus on earth through the body of Mary wife of Joseph.

CHAPTER 20: HOLY SPIRIT CHANGED FROM FEMALE TO MALE?

C.1 There are many reasons for this but in general it is all about demonic control of the church system and thus the people by making the popes just like the Caesar's of Rome or absolute monarchs who could decide who lived and who died. By around 300 AD there was a lot of division amongst the churches, and they had different belief systems. The key to the change from feminine to masculine was when the emperor of Rome Constantine in 312 AD embraced the church in Rome or that version of Christianity.

C.2 In 324 AD at a meeting of Nicaea held by Constantine female bishops were banned as were many of the Christian sects such as the popular Marcion Faith and New Prophecy churches. The Holy Spirit was known as feminine in the original Hebrew or Syriac which was a local dialect around Jerusalem. The Holy Spirit stayed feminine in the Eastern, Orthodox Empire.

C.3 The gospels were translated first into Greek from Hebrew and then into Latin. The Holy Spirit was feminine in the Hebrew language but it became neutral in Greek and then masculine when it was translated into Latin.

C.4 That was the problem. At the end of the 4th century the Eastern Orthodox churches started to change the feminine Holy Spirit Mother to masculine as they were afraid of Rome. The demonic control of religion by the Catholic church made it very dangerous to even mention that the Holy Spirit was feminine so many scribes got busy *altering the texts*.

C.5 There is a lot of evidence for this. A lot of people who did not agree with the Laodicean edict in 364 AD were simply burned at the stake. That practice continued for well over 1000 years.

C.6 There was a couple and their children burned at the stake in London in 1601.Why? Just for reading a Bible in English instead of Latin! Talk about demonic control of religion. 'The powers that be' have always been guilty of this kind of control. 'He who controls knowledge, controls the people'. That is one of their mottos.

Acts 7:51-53 - " Ye stiff-necked and uncircumcised in heart and ears, ye do always resist the Holy Ghost: as your fathers did, so do ye. Who have received the law by the 'disposition of angels' and have not kept it.

C.7 This simply means that the Pharisees of Jesus time got their laws from 'fallen angels' or devils and not from the Spirit of God. Now how did that happen and when in history? Now that is a very good question. The big question is how and when that all started. After all Moses was a good guy and brought in the 10 Commandments directly from the finger of God on Mount Sinai.

C.8 So, what went wrong after Moses brought in all of God's laws? It is not the actual laws but the spirit by which they are implemented which can be twisted to do evil as the Pharisees did in murdering their own Saviour Jesus Christ, the Son of God. The demonic side always resist the Spirit of God.

Acts 7.51 Ye stiff-necked and uncircumcised in heart and ears, ye do always resist the Holy Ghost: as your fathers did so do ye.

CHAPTER 21: THE PROPHET OF GOD

C.1 The prophet has to more or less be between two worlds, or in between two worlds, or in two worlds at the same time, one foot in one and one foot in the other. He has to take in what God is showing him in the world of the spirit and then relate it back to earth by describing the visions, revelations or messages that he is receiving from the Lord, so that others can benefit from them also. The prophet looks up to the heavenly realm of the Spirit to receive messages from God's Son Jesus which are being passed on to Him by God's wonderful Holy Spirit Mother.

TOMORROW'S WONDERFUL WORLD

C.2 I looked into the future and what did I see?

A wonderful world that's happy and free!

Where lions and tigers are friendly and tame.

Where children can kiss and not be ashamed!

Where beautiful maidens are loving and kind.

And no one is in a hurry there is plenty of time!

Where there is no pollution No oil or gas,

And people more slowly Never too fast!

Where no one is rich and no one is poor,

When the world is at peace

And there's no more war!

C.3 SUMMARY It is1740 years since the Catholic church took the knowledge away about the Holy Spirit being female at the edict of Laodicea in 364 AD. It is more than the Holy Spirit being mentioned as a feminine expression. She is Mother God and Wisdom (Sophia in Greek) She is the wife of God the Father and Jesus is their Son. One can find evidence of this in 'Wisdom of Solomon', Proverbs 8, Sirach, Secrets of Enoch and countless other books of the Early Christians. It is true that all the ancient Hebrews knew that the Holy Spirit is feminine and a female being in nature.

C.4 As one woman wrote to me some time ago 'How could an 'all masculine' Trinity possibly have designed a woman?' I told her that she was perfectly correct. Only a woman could design a woman. Knowing that God the Father is masculine and His wife is the female Holy Spirit Mother makes perfect sense. Their son is Jesus. The Bible shows a perfect example in *Genesis 1.26-28* when God stated 'Let us make man in our image and male and female created He them. Who was God talking to unless it was His wife the Holy Spirit as they went on to make people both male and female.

C.5 You can see the Pre-Creation talking about all this in the 2nd Book of Enoch. Spiritually speaking just as it is possible to talk to and get answers from Jesus it is also possible to talk with the Holy Spirit Mother and hear from her also. She is a wonderful 'Goddess Mother' and a true Comforter. Everyone who loves Jesus should get to also know her. Solomon in the Bible also stated this exact same thing 1000 years before Jesus our Savior was born.

C. 6 I have also recently written about *Holy Spirit Mother in my new book 'Secrets of Enoch Insights'*

Please see my *new website and BLOG: www.insightspublication.com*

C.7 As A Christian Missionary: In investigating what others have written about receiving the Holy Spirit (Mother) I am shocked to see that they don't talk about the importance of receiving the Holy Spirit to have the *power to be a witness* for Christ. They talk about receiving the Holy Spirit to do good works, but they don't talk in the language of a *disciple of Christ*, who is supposed to be dedicated to *telling others about Jesus* the Son of the Holy Spirit and God the Father.

C.8 We as true Christians are supposed to be telling others about the simplicity of Salvation and of receiving the power of the Holy Ghost. The Holy Ghost (Mother) is given to those who obey Jesus command to 'Go Ye into all the world and preach the Gospel unto every creature'.

C.9 The Holy Ghost was not given to people just to go to church buildings and have fellowship with other Christians. The job of a true Christian is to be a witness for Christ like the early disciples were. Most of so-called Christianity has totally lost its meaning in modern times.

C.10 In this book I have mostly been mentioning about the importance of knowing that the Holy Spirit is our spiritual Mother and the Mother of Jesus the Messiah. However, I must also point out the importance of telling others about Jesus, so that they can be truly saved and if possible and filled with His Holy Spirit so that Jesus and the Holy Spirt Mother can take care of that soul. It makes me sad to see how that the churches don't seem to know what being a true Christian is apart from a tradition of good works.

C.11 Steve (Author) As a missionary for the past 51 years, the greatest joy I have personally experienced has been in praying with others to receive Jesus into their hearts and inspiring them to pray to get filled with the Holy Spirit. The problem is that I see the churches pray with people to get saved mostly by tradition of baptism, but mostly they don't encourage their members to get out and tell others about Jesus. By so doing their 'converts' will not grow spiritually.

C.12 The Holy Spirit Mother remains with the new convert to nurture them, but especially with those that obey Jesus command to 'Go into all the world and preach the gospel unto every creature. That means getting out where you are and telling others about Jesus and Salvation by the grace of God.

CHAPTER 22: MY PERSONAL TESTIMONIES ABOUT MEETING THE HOLY SPIRIT MOTHER

C.1 I was thinking about different times when I have experienced the Holy Spirit Mother. I was praying and talking to the Holy Spirit Mother and She told me that she takes care of all of God's children around the world and that She visits them when they need her or reach out for Her help. Many people are important to God and He has pre-chosen them and knows that they will end up following Him. He is just waiting for them to make the right choice.

C.2 The Holy Spirit Mother patiently hovers and waits until She can help them find salvation in her Son Jesus. He waits patiently and lets humans pass through difficulties and sorrows until realize their need for Christ.

C.3 Some must pass through sickness or accidents or difficulties or loneliness or heartbreak or other things until they realise that Jesus is their Lord and saviour. Who is it that directs people. The Holy Spirit delights in people. Being with the sons of men and daughters. She loves people and She goes wherever She is wanted and needed. Some people receive Her and others reject her. She cannot stick around those who reject Her.

C.4 That is the Mother the Holy Spirit the spirit of love and kindness and comfort. She helps you and as soon as you show interest in Her Son Jesus she comes and helps you to find Him. She helps those who are hungry for the truth but the rich and full she sends empty away – the ones who think that they can do without her.

C.5 Holy Spirit talking to my wife recently: 'So yes, I was there that moment when you got saved and when you had your serious accident, I was there to comfort you, wrapping a comforting blanket of My Spirit of love around you. That is why it says that the Father and the Holy Ghost and the Son of God are *One*.

1 Jn 5.7 For there are three that bear record in heaven, the Father, the Word, and the Holy Ghost: and these three are one.

C.6 They are there for each other and they help each other. They help the people, and they work together. You got saved because someone told you how to get saved and you said 'Yes, I want that'. I will receive Jesus into my heart. I will believe on Him.' You prayed and you were hungry, and you were praying for the truth. Help me Lord I need the truth. I don't know why I am here and what I am doing in this life. What is my purpose? A short time later you met someone, and they told you about righteousness and the truth about Jesus. That is when Jesus came into your heart and when I the Holy Spirit Mother wrapped my arms around you. You have a few stories about how I helped you. I come in many forms. I come as a spirit, that you can't see but you can feel Me. I come as a fire, and I come as a Dove of the Holy Spirit. Tongues of Fire and I come as a Dove. Sometimes I appear through the eyes of certain people. They don't know it, but I can shine right through certain peoples' eyes as light or fire.

C.7 My wife was praying and asking the Holy Spirit Mother: 'What about the times when my husband Stephen saw a woman who looked at him with eyes of light and fire and love. Was that you? Answer from Holy Spirit Mother: 'At times when Stephen cannot see things spiritual so clearly, I have indeed showed up in person'.

C.8 The truth be said when I first had the above experience as mentioned by my wife, the woman in question was too far away for me to notice what she actually looked like. Somehow, she projected a fiery stream of light from her eyes directly at me and I was at the time driving towards her car that was approaching a T junction that I was soon to pass by. It was a momentary thing. I was not the only one to see it. My son who was also in our car also saw her. I did experience this happening again on 4 other occasions. On one of the occasions, I saw the woman close up, and her eyes transmitted that same amazing love and compassion and caring spirit. Once you have met Her, you have a strong desire to meet Her again. She is Wisdom and the Holy Spirit Mother.

C.9 Meeting the Holy Spirit Mother: On Another occasion when I met her it was very odd. I was driving downtown on a Saturday morning with two of our teenage daughters when again I came along the narrow road of a T- Junction meeting a main road. Suddenly, the 4-wheel drive car coming along the main road slowed down and stopped on the main road to let me in and pass into the main road. The woman turned and looked at me and she had those same eyes of light. The effect it had on me was to make me totally victorious in spirit as before this happened, I was not so victorious in spirit. On yet another occasion, I was having a coffee in Starbucks with my teenage son and daughter when a woman passed the long glass windows of the café and suddenly stopped and looked directly at me. Her eyes were full of light and love. My daughter blurted out 'Dad is there something you are not telling us about this woman'? I stammered 'It is the same woman that I have now seen 3 times during the past week. Note: I did not know at the time, but within 10 days of these strange sightings of this very beautiful woman, I ended up in the intensive care at the hospital having chronic anaemia and I need 4 blood transfusions. I stayed in the hospital for 7 days only PTL.

C.10 There was another occasion when my son met one of the 'maidens' or angels sent by the Holy Spirit Mother. I was supposed to pick my son up at the train station. When I got there, I saw my son coming down the stairs from the train station. He was talking with a pretty girl, and she sort of disappeared into the background. I asked my son who the girl was, but he acted sort of bewildered as though not having understood his experience with her. When I said to him, I think she is that angel I have been seeing recently, but in a younger form. What did she say to you? But he acted sort of mesmerized and had no explanation for her behaviour. However, I knew that it was indeed the same angel that I had seen before. Obviously, my son, not understanding the spiritual situation that he passed through. It must have been that the message was meant for me. In looking at those angelic experiences that I had in 2010. It was as if she was sent to me, as God was very concerned about my health, as I was in fact very ill at the time but did not know it. It only became clear some days following this last angelic incident. I have had quite a few angelic experiences in my life, but it is like being in a bubble at the time when these things happen as no one else around the scene seems to see it or understand it. Like the scene in the Bible where Jesus met Paul in a vision on the road to Damascus. It stated that those companions of Paul heard a voice, but they didn't see anything and they were right next to Paul when he saw the vision. Visions are normally personal occurrences.

ACTS 22.6-9 And it came to pass, that, as I made my journey, and was come nigh unto Damascus about noon, suddenly there shone from heaven a great light round about me. And I fell unto the ground, and heard a voice saying unto me, Saul, Saul, why persecute thou me? And I answered, Who art thou, Lord? And he said unto me, I am Jesus of Nazareth, whom thou persecute. And they that were with me saw indeed the light and were afraid; but they heard not the voice of him that spake to me.

C.11 My wife was asking if it was the same woman that I saw in my visions every single time? I explained that no it was not always the same physical woman although the spirit shining through was always the same spirit which I at first related to others was a female angel or even my own guardian angel but that later on or I should say recently I came to understand more fully that she was actually the Holy Spirit Mother.

C.12 I am flattered to know that she loves and cares for me so well. I am convinced that the same angel can shine through almost anybody although they personally are probably totally unaware of what is happening.

C.13 In the case of my visions on the 1st occasion I could not see what the physical woman looked like but only experience her long-distance look of fire and light. On one occasion I saw the woman close up and on yet another she was as a teenager.

C.14 So, the spirits can appear through many forms of humans. I have had other amazing experiences with angels. My first experience was when I was 21.

CHAPTER 23: HEARING FROM GOD

C.1 All the Verses About Wisdom in The Bible and Living For God.

Proverbs 2.8 For the Lord giveth Wisdom: out of His mouth cometh knowledge and understanding.

Proverbs 1.2 "To know wisdom and instruction; to perceive the words of understanding;"

Proverbs 1.5 A wise *man* will hear, and will increase learning; and a man of understanding shall attain unto wise counsels:

C.2 HEARING FROM GOD: I find it amazing that many sites on the net acknowledge that the Proverbs refer to Wisdom as feminine, but they just refuse to get the point. Their answer is well we just don't know why Proverbs talks about Wisdom as feminine, as the Bible does not tell us why.

C.3 It is so sad to see that so many so-called Christians don't actually have a living relationship with God, otherwise they would be getting lots of answers from Heaven.

C.4 From my experience, most religious people are afraid of hearing from God, Jesus and the Holy Spirit, in case they tell them something that they think that they can't handle. The result has been that most religionists simple don't really know God. So many have cut themselves off from the truth by excluding prophecy in their lives. Without prophecy, you also won't get visions and prophetic dreams from heaven or even daily answers to your questions.

C.5 I remember so well when I was young and went to a boarding school where one was compelled to go to chapel every day...but it was totally dead spiritually and in general that is how most religions are - spiritually dead. Just an imitation Christianity but denying the power thereof.

2 Timothy 3.5,7 Having a form of godliness but denying the power thereof: from such turn away. Ever learning, and never able to come to the knowledge of the truth.

C.6 Our relationship with God is supposed to be an active and two-way relationship. Otherwise. it is a dead relationship and of no purpose.

Sadly, most religionists are deliberately 'willingly ignorant' of so many things that go on all around them and in God's world. Religionists tend to cook up intellectual answers that do not really address the spiritual issues involved. In order to be truly spiritual you have to do what Jesus said in *Matthew chapter 18*.

Matthew 18.3 And said, Verily I say unto you, 'Except ye be converted, and become as little children, ye shall not enter into the kingdom of heaven'.

John 3.3 Jesus answered and said unto him, Verily, verily, I say unto thee, Except a man be born again, he cannot see the kingdom of God.

C.7 Apparently, 70% of pastors in the USA today do not follow a biblical perspective. So, what about the rest of the world?

2 Peter 3.5 For this they willingly are ignorant, that by the word of God the heavens were of old, and the earth standing out of the water and in the water.

C.8 Wisdom is given to us by God the Father and by Jesus and they send wisdom to us by the Holy Spirit Mother. It is just that simple. These 3 are One and agree in One.

1 John 5.7 "For there are three that bear record in heaven, the Father, the Word, and the Holy Ghost: and these three are one."

C.9 What is important is that our motive in life is to help others and in my case as a missionary for over 50 years my job has been to tell others about Jesus and how wonderful He really is. Teach others to get saved by receiving Jesus into their hearts and lives. I have been very much helped by His Mother the Holy Spirit Mother.

Revelation 3.20 Behold I stand at the door and knock, if any man hear my voice and open the door I will come into him and sup with him and he with Me.

John 3.16 For God so loved the world, that he gave his only begotten Son, that whosoever believeth in him should not perish, but have everlasting life.

Acts 1.8 "But ye shall receive power, after that the Holy Ghost is come upon you: and ye shall be witnesses unto me both in Jerusalem, and in all Judaea, and in Samaria, and unto the uttermost part of the earth."

C.10 Our job as Christians is to 'stay in God's spirit' as others have correctly said. What does this mean? Well, it means being dedicated to Jesus and His Word every day. It means putting Jesus and the Word of God first in our lives before anything else.

Acts 5.32 And we are his witnesses of these things; and so is also the Holy Ghost, whom God hath given to them that obey him.

C.11 Of course, this also includes prayer and praise and making an effort to hear from God daily.

Mathew 7.7 Ask, and it shall be given you; seek, and ye shall find; knock, and it shall be opened unto you: For every one that asks receives; and he that seeks finds; and to him that knocks it shall be opened.

C.12 God is certainly going to give to His children what they need and what is good for them.

The Holy Spirit Mother is the one who helps God's children or Jesus's followers to stay close to God and to dedicate one's life to Him.

C.13 Another very important point is for each of us to learn to behave in a godly manner and not be soon angry at others or soon impatient.

Galatians 5.22-23 The fruit of the spirit is love, joy, peace, longsuffering, gentleness, goodness, faith, meekness temperance against such there is no law.

James 1.5 If any of you lack **wisdom**, let him ask of God, that giveth to all men liberally, and upbraids not; and it shall be given him.

This clearly shows us how to obtain godly wisdom and that is from God. God sends His Spirit of love to teach us.

Proverbs 1.7 The fear of the LORD is the beginning of knowledge: but fools despise **wisdom** and instruction. It constantly amazes me how this world in general just does not get the point of life and having godly wisdom.

Proverbs 2.1-22 My son, if thou wilt receive my words, and hide my commandments with thee.

Psalm 111.10 The fear of the LORD is the beginning of **wisdom**: a good understanding have all they that do his commandments: his praise endures for ever.

C.14 To be in the fear of the Lord is the key to wisdom.

Ecclesiastes 7.12 For **wisdom** is a defence, and money is a defence: but the excellency of knowledge is, that **wisdom** giveth life to them that have it.

C.15 What is the point of money if it cannot make you wiser?

Isaiah 11.2 And the spirit of the LORD shall rest upon him, the spirit of **wisdom** and understanding, the spirit of counsel and might, the spirit of knowledge and of the fear of the LORD.

1 Timothy 2.4 Who will have all men to be saved, and to come unto the knowledge of the truth.

Matthew 7.7-8 Ask, and it shall be given you; seek, and ye shall find; knock, and it shall be opened unto you:

C.16 WISDOM OF THE WORLD

1 Corinthians 3.19-20 For the wisdom of this world is foolishness with God. For it is written, He taketh the wise in their own craftiness.

Proverbs 4.1-27 Hear, ye children, the instruction of a father, and attend to know understanding.

Romans 1.22-25 Professing themselves to be wise, they became fools.

James 3.15-18 This wisdom descends not from above, but is earthly, sensual, devilish.

C.17 GODLY WISDOM

2 Chronicles 1.7-12 In that night did God appear unto Solomon, and said unto him, 'Ask what I shall give thee'.

James 3.17 But the wisdom that is from above is first pure, then peaceable, gentle, and easy to be intreated, full of mercy and good fruits, without partiality, and without hypocrisy.

Proverbs 16.16 How much better is it to get wisdom than gold and to get understanding rather to be chosen than silver.

Proverb 13.10 Only by pride cometh contention:

but with the well advised is wisdom.

Proverbs 19.8 He that gets wisdom loves his own soul and that keeps understanding shall find good.

1 Corinthians 3.18 Let no man deceive himself. If any man among you seems to be wise in this world, let him become a fool, that he may be wise.

Psalm 90.12 So teach us to number our days, that we may apply our hearts to wisdom.

Matthew 7.24 Therefore whosoever heareth these sayings of mine, and doeth them, I will liken him unto a wise man, which built his house upon a rock.

Proverbs 15.33 The fear of the Lord is the instruction of wisdom; and before honour is humility.

Proverbs 11.2 When pride cometh, then cometh shame:

but with the lowly is wisdom.

CHAPTER 24: SPIRITUAL HAPPENINGS

C.1 Have you ever noticed that when you have dreams that it all suddenly all dissolves away and you end up forgetting the whole dream. I have had a few rare exceptions where I could still remember the dream later in the same day. If it was an important or significant dream, I had to write it down right away or else it would seem be completely lost.

C.2 As in regard to the spirit world and the difference between the heavenly beings and races of humans already up in heaven. Those beings are always in the 'presence of the Lord' and feel the full influence of His wonderful eternal light. They know the full truth of heaven and its wonders and beauties, and they are as an intimate family with God the Father, Holy Spirit Mother and with Christ as His Bride.

C.3 I know the total fulfilment of the Bride of Christ has not yet come, but will soon come as Jesus returns the 2nd time.

C.4 It is important to believe in Love, as God is Love. Love gives the ability to create. Love gives wisdom. Love gives the feeding Word of God.

I really love Holy Spirit Mother as She gives me so much love for the Word of God -her Son Jesus.

C.5 When we look at the 4 Gospels and see how Jesus only went everywhere doing good and being kind and always loving and protecting His hungry sheep: but also protecting them from the wolves (Pharisees) with his amazing answers to their questions and accusations.

Who could be more wonderful than Jesus? The very Son of the Holy Spirit Mother. I believe that so far until this point in time, that fact that the Holy Spirit Mother has been hidden from most people since 364 AD has not been the 'end of the world' so to speak, as long as people do get saved and receive Jesus Her Son so that at least they can get saved and have eternal life.

C.6 However, I do believe that it will be the Holy Spirit Mother who is largely in charge in the coming age of the Millenium.

The Golden Age when there shall be no more war. Peace on earth will have been restored. The everlasting Prince of peace shall reign to the ends of the earth. A wonderful new age where no one is too rich, and no one is too poor. Everyone will have enough. In the current life on earth unfortunately Satan the prince of this world, as Satan himself declared unto Jeus the Christ when his was on earth: 'This world is delivered unto me, and I give it to whomsoever I will.'

Luke 4:6 And the devil said unto him, All this power will I give thee, and the glory of them: for that is delivered unto me; and to whomsoever I will I give it.

C.7 The good news is that Satan has usurped this physical world but that he will soon lose his position when Christ the Savior returns the 2nd time to redeem the earth and set-up His coming glorious Millennial kingdom together with His glorified saints, angels and other beings from heaven.

CHAPTER 25: LUCIFER AND THE FALLEN ANGELS

C.1 It goes all the way back to the fallen angels as to why the gender of the Holy Spirit being feminine was deliberately altered. and I think one has to go back to Pre-Flood times in order to fully understand the real problem.

There has been a strong hatred of women throughout history as they have been blamed for many things in the past, where society has tried to push women into subservient roles in society because of religions. Why did this happen? Is there a strong reason? I think it all stems from Pre-Flood times and that men after the Great Flood did not want their women to behave as the *daughters of Cain* ever again. They also did not want the women to abandon the normal human men in favour of 'Fallen angels' (devils) as happened in **Genesis 6 and Enoch 6, Jasher,5, Jubilees 4.**

C.2 I also think that there is a strong argument as to why the Fallen angels and Satan ended up hating women. It was because they hated the female Holy Spirit Mother. This is the reason why the knowledge about the Holy Spirit being female or Mother God *is* deliberately hidden. It is the *Holy Ghost* who drives demons out of people through the Word of God. (Jesus)

John 1.1-3 In the beginning was the Word and the Word was with God and was God. The same was in the beginning with God. Without him was nothing made that was made.

GOD THE FATHER DOES HAVE A WIFE?

C.3 I must also state here that it is essential to realize that of course God the Father has a wife and companion in the Holy Spirit Mother and always has done. These are eternal values. As other scholars have rightly stated, when you look at the Bible through the lenses of the Holy Spirit being the Mother in the so-called Trinity everything else makes perfect sense.

C.4 Now why on earth would this information be withheld from believers for the past 1600+ years until now?

Did you know that Origen who started the Catholic church and whose books were the basis of the Catholic church religion and who incidentally lived in the 3rd century A.D. warned the Catholic church that if they did not change their ways, they would become infested with demons or the children of the Fallen angels otherwise known as the 'disembodied spirits' of the giants.

DEMONIC BEHAVIOUR OF THE CHURCH

C.5 It would seem that that is exactly what happened from the 4th century onwards as the Catholic church burned at the stake anyone who did not agree with their religious dictums of the moment. In other words, they were controlled by devils.

The Catholic church has a lot of blood on their hands including that of Joan of Arc. They martyred her and 20 years later declared her as one of their saints.

Between 300-400 AD at the council of Laodicea women were banned from being bishops and spiritual leaders. Many were burned alive in their own churches for not following papal orders.

THE ORIGINAL FALL OF THE ANGELS 500 YEARS AFTER CREATION

C.6 Satan and 'The Fallen angels' chose the ways of total rebellion against God, but they obviously were not too smart after all, as their plans all failed. The fallen angels thought that they would go down to earth to cohabitate with the beautiful women on the earth and begat children by them. However, they forgot one very important thing. Creation is by God the Father *and by God the Mother* as well as by Jesus their Son.

According to Genesis God the Father and God the Mother were talking together when in Genesis 1 God stated:

Genesis 1 'Let us make man in our image and male and female created He them.

God was obviously talking with a female and that was the Holy Spirit Mother.

C.7 The Fallen angels left out 'God the Mother', who was the one who created all the females in God's Creation. Angels were not supposed to mingle with human women and something went very wrong when they co-habited with the human women. When the Fallen angels had sex with the women on the earth, that is why they could only have sons and *no daughters*. Perhaps the angelic DNA was overly masculine, as the angels were not supposed to have sex with human women who were only temporary beings and not eternal. No wonder their sons the giants went crazy and berserk with no giants around that were female.

Book of Enoch 15.2 Wherefore have Ye left the high, holy and eternal heaven, and lain with women, and defiled yourselves with the daughters of men and taken to yourselves wives and done like the children of earth and begotten giants for your sons.

C.8 Notice that it only says sons and not 'sons and daughters'. Why could the Fallen angels only have sons with the women on the earth?

1) It was disobedience against God.

2) It takes the dominance of XX Chromosomes to have a baby girl. A boy is XY chromosome.

3) Without the dominance of the female cells, which involves the help of the Holy Spirit Mother who is in charge of the feminine side of Creation the fallen angels could only have sons and *no daughters*.

4) The angels were eternal beings and the human women were temporal beings and something simply did not work properly because of the very serious disobedience to God that was involved, God could not bless the Fallen angels and their plans to procreate.

5) Their sons the giants had no giant females to procreate together with.

6) Our God is a God of Creation and that partly involves the feminine Holy

Spirit Mother for creation to work properly. Well, that is my take on it.

C.9 After co-habiting with the women for a while, then the Fallen angels started mating with animals and other creatures and created chimeras. This was possible as angels are shapeshifters. They also did this with other creatures. Such a total horror and aberration of God's original Creation. The evil spirit world is now therefore very perverse, and they do not according to nature, or stick to male and female relationships.

C.10 This is also why our planet is having such problems to this day. Everything of real value is being destroyed. It used to be simple that a man is a man and woman is a woman, but now they can't even define what a woman is!

C.11 This is 'newspeak' as mentioned by George Orwell in his dystopian book '1984'. If things continue the way that they are going one day people won't even be able to understand each other's speech as all the words will mean something else. What utter madness!

THE COSMIC BATTLE OF JESUS (*HUMILITY*) AGAINST SATAN (*PRIDE*)

C.12 Ever since time immemorial, this battle has been constantly waged. So where did it all start? It has been stated that before the physical creation, there existed a heavenly realm which was inhabited by spirit beings of all types. All originally were obedient to God. God realized however, in His infinite wisdom, that ultimately it would be better if everyone followed His orders, not because they felt forced to, or that they were so afraid not to obey God's every whim, but *by choice*.

C.13 The Bible tells us clearly, that God Himself, at the essence of His being is Love. We also know that Jesus is the opposite of Satan, and is the Spirit of Humility, and so also is His Holy Spirit Mother. She is Love.

We are told by the scriptures, that God has simply always been, and that He is the Great 'I am that I am'. We have also learnt from scripture that Jesus is the Word of God, and it was Jesus along with the Holy Spirit of God, that were responsible for the physical creation. Apparently, they were hindered in the creation story by Satan himself at some time or other. Avak the Oriental Mystic prophet stated that Satan destroyed God's original Creation in the 'Great Heavenly Rebellion' by both himself and the Fallen Angels. Then God recreated order out of the chaos that the Devil had made in his anger and rebellion.

WHY DID SATAN REBEL AGAINST GOD IN THE FIRST PLACE?

C.14 'Long, long ago, Lucifer stood at the right hand of God. He bore the light. He was not the light, but he held the light on high for all the inhabitants of the universe to see. He was the standard bearer, the mightiest of all archangels, and he exercised some of the power of Almighty God Himself in helping to rule the universe. Then pride took its grip. Though he held such a high and honoured position, Lucifer was no longer satisfied with bearing the light of God. He wanted to be God Himself.

WHAT TRIGGERED SATAN'S FALL?

C.15 Apparently, according to a very interesting prophecy that I had the privilege of reading, it all started when God came to present His 'Only Begotten Son Jesus' to all the Hosts of Heaven. Satan thought that he himself being the mightiest of all archangels, should be the next in line for this honour:

'Infested with pride, he refused to listen to God. He refused to listen to the other angelic forces and to the Heavenly inhabitants. He refused any, and all help to see the right. Because he refused to admit he was wrong and say he was sorry, because he chose to hold on to his pride, strong delusion set in. Refusing to humble himself before a powerful and awesome God, his own loving, patient and understanding Father, Lucifer fell. He altered the course of his own destiny. He didn't *have* to fall; he *chose* to fall. He chose his own course, all because of his lust for power and his proud refusal to choose the humble way.

This is when insanity took tight hold on Lucifer. This is when of his own choosing he was transformed from Lucifer, the bearer of light, to Satan, the Devil, the father of lies. This is when the long trek began. From the moment of that decision, he set out on his hostile mission. From that time on, he set out to live at enmity with God, His creation, and His children.'

THE FALL OF THE FALLEN ANGELS

C.16 When Satan fell, he tried to persuade others of the angels to go with him. Those who accepted his lies became poisoned, drawn away by their own desires. Therefore, pride took hold and they were overcome. Hence, Satan and his band of dark angels began to roam the Earth. It wasn't long before they realized if they were to win others to their side, they would have to come up with a plan, a scheme of some sort, something that would convince others to join them rather than continue being loyal and dedicated to the loving and just ways of the Heavenly Father. Having declared his own independence from righteous rule, Satan went into business for himself. His goal was to win as many others over to his side as he could. His purpose was to spread his own insanity and delusion to others; to prove that you could live without God, that you could in fact *be* God.

C.17 This is how Satan's plan came into being. That is when he began laying the foundation for his counterfeit kingdom; that is when the plan of his great deception began. Sadly, the precepts of his plan thrive in the world today. They touch every corner of the world. His philosophy is booming throughout society at large.'

FALLING LOWER & LOWER

C.18 But step by step Satan is being forced down to the ground, lower and lower he is being driven down each day, and it's killing him. He is king over all the children of pride. He loves to establish himself and his kingdom in high places, and among the rich and powerful of the Earth, where he can control the most people. Ultimately, he wants to control everything and everyone. He mistook God's assigning of significant duties and responsibilities to His creations as a sign of God's weakness and not His love and transcendent power and majesty."

JOB.41:34 He beholds all high things: he is a king over all the children of pride.

MORE ABOUT THE FALLEN ANGELS

C.19 This is an important topic that I didn't think that I was going to write about in a book about the Holy Spirit Mother. Why is it essential to mention the Fallen angels and their offspring the Giants in pre-Flood times? Well, I think it is very important to know what was happening in the Pre-Flood world and for others to know the Creation story as well as how evil started and what repercussions that it led to.

It is also one of the reasons why the truth about the Holy Spirit Mother being a feminine being has been deliberately hidden from mankind for thousands of years.

According to the Bible in Genesis chapter 6 as well as the ancient Book of Enoch chapter 6. Not to mention Jasher chapter 4 and Jubilees Chapter 5 certain of the angels of God fell at the orders of Satan and came down to the earth to procreate with the women on the earth. According to the Lost Books of Adam and Eve the fallen angels went to be with the licentious daughters of Cain at least initially. These licentious daughters of Cain participated in wild orgies and thus attracted evil spirits. How did that all begin? Well, that began with Satan in the Garden of Eden and then with the Fallen angels coming down to have sex with the 'daughters of men'.

C.20 It is this side of things that is related to the Holy Spirit Mother. This is also the reason why the demons and devils hate her and the feminine side of things in humans. Why could the angels only father sons with the human women? Now there is a question we would all like to know the answer to. Well, that is my idea, conclusion and hypothesis. What makes me come to this conclusion? Firstly, the Fallen angels were not supposed to have sex with human women.

C.21 I believe that since the fallen angels could have sex with the women on earth then there obviously must be female angels as well. The Fallen angels should not have abandoned the female angels in heaven. Why did they? What is the difference? Because they were angelic beings or eternal beings their male DNA must have been too dominant when having intercourse with human women and thus caused an imbalance in the human women's wombs.

C.22 The fruit of the women or earth's wombs after having sex with angels was to only give birth to male children and they grew to enormous size which also caused a big problem for mankind. The children of the Fallen angels not only became monstrous giants but also cannibals, who started devouring mankind.

C.23 If you studied my last book *'Secrets of Enoch Insights'* which is based on the 2nd Book of Enoch you will discover the amazing truth that eventually Satan and the Fallen angels get thrown into the Lake of Fire.

C.24 Strangely, in the 2nd *Book of Enoch* we also see universal reconciliation as after Satan and the Fallen angels have been thrown into the Lake of fire they are challenged by Enoch to cry out to God for their deliverance and they finally do and everything from then on changes for good. Amazing end to the story. However, all the creations of the *Fallen angels* they the fallen angels are commanded to destroy including all the spirits of the *Giants* who later became the evil spirits and demons according to the Hebrew Book of Jubilees during the time right after the Great Flood of Noah. The angels will eventually return unto God but *not* all of their abominable creations such as the *Giants* and all the hybrid creatures that they made.

C.25 As I have mentioned throughout this book the 'powers that be' have tried to hide the truth concerning the *Holy Spirit Mother* and also the history of Satan and the Fallen angels also as well as the origin of the demons and devils. The satanic side is very much afraid of God's Creation. I suppose because they feel left out of it and only in a prison whether the underneath or the lower dimensions and Satan always thought that he should have been the 'big honcho' and not God. Since Satan got thrown out of heaven and then all of his Fallen angels, he lived in a la-la land of thinking that he is the boss of everything when clearly he is not. So Satan and the Fallen angels keep living in their unhappy delusion that they will someday win the fight and defeat God. They really are pretty stupid to think that they can fight against God and all of his angels and angelized saints.

C.26 Another topic is why didn't God forgive the Fallen angels when they first fell from heaven and were weeping in front of Enoch begging him to ask God for their forgiveness? To which God said a firm No! Why? Because they had wrought so much destruction of human beings upon the earth in Pre-Flood times. God told them that they would be imprisoned for 7000 to 10,000 years. Wouldn't it have been a lot easier for all of us if God had forgiven them in the beginning of Creation so that our planet didn't have to end up the way it is today -in total chaos, war, destruction, famine, starvation, floods and much more? Of course, God Himself has a very good answer to this question.

'WHO WAS LUCIFER'S MOTHER'- AND SUMMARY?

C.27 *Lucifer* means *'light-bearer'* whilst he was still working for God until he was changed into Satan meaning the Devil and Lucifer. Satan means Destroyer.

The king of pride is a destructive and destroying adversary. Satan is a master of deception, and he destroys through misinformation.

Revelation 9:11 names him Abaddon (Destruction) and Apollyon (Destroyer).

"And they had a king over them, *which is* the angel of the bottomless pit, whose name in the Hebrew tongue *is* Abaddon, but in the Greek tongue hath *his* name Apollyon."

C.28 This knowledge has been deliberately hidden for a very long time. It would appear that Lucifer does not want people to know who his mother was. Did you know that the British Medical Foundation just banned the word mother in their so-called modern deviant way of thinking. I was just checking what the religious people say and they tell the story that God is the one who created the angels and that they did not need to have a mother because angels are not physical beings. That argument is not true to God's Creation.

The religious people really don't' seem to have a clue and have no answers as to the true nature of the spirit world. Others point to evil goddesses for the answer but what is the truth?

C.29 Another example of getting rid of the feminine. This is a shocker I know, but in discussing this my new book *Wisdom Insights* and talking with my wife about the Holy Spirit Mother my wife mentioned how I have been writing about and asking the question 'why does Satan hate the feminine side' of humans and I have mentioned what I thought could be the reasons but *she has suggested something far more important* in answering this very question. The Bible tells us in the book of Job:

Job 1.7 Now there was a day when the sons of God (angels) came to present themselves before God and Satan (Lucifer) was among them

C.30 My wife stated 'well now that we know that God the Father has a wife as in the Holy Spirit Mother then that must mean that She is Mother of all living. She also must have been the *mother* of Lucifer otherwise the sons of God mentioned in *Job 1.7* could not be sons of God.

C.31 I have put forth the argument in this book that *everyone has a mother*. Male and female are spiritual eternal values not just physical. The religious people just try to avoid the topic or explain it all away as God is creator and there is no mother in heaven they say and thus there is no male and female in the spirit world. Everything in the spirit world we know nothing about and don't care either -they say. That is such a mindless position to take. In general, the churches don't like anyone thinking outside of their church box of narrow-minded religion.

C.32 I have mentioned that the so-called religious *Trinity* is false, as one of the beings should be feminine and the three of them cannot all be masculine. That goes against nature in both the physical and spirit world. It was Satan who was behind the Catholic church who got rid of the Holy Spirit Mother being in the Trinity in 364 A.D.at the infamous 'Council of Laodicea.

C.33 Once one realizes that fact then the main issue of this book as to *why has the feminine side of humanity been suppressed* in the religious fields becomes apparent.

C.34 Why did the Catholic church ban the knowledge of the Holy Spirit Mother in 364 AD at the Edict of Laodicea.

C.35 Why did they also ban the Books of Enoch at that same time? It was because it exposed the Fallen angels and the origin of sexual perversions.

C.36 I have also stated that in my opinion the reason the demonic side hates the feminine is because they themselves are largely perverts. How did that happen? It happened when the reprobate Fallen Angels came down to the earth and had sex with the licentious daughters of Cain.

C.37 I have stated that according to scripture Cain was a son of Satan:

1 John 3.12 "Not as Cain, *who* was of that *wicked* one (*Satan*), and slew his brother. And wherefore slew he him? Because his own works were evil, and his brother's righteous.

C.38 When the licentious daughters of Cain got pregnant with the Fallen angels, for some reason they could only have **sons** who became the monstrous carnivorous giants. They could not have daughters! Why?

C.39 When their sons the giants died they disappeared into the negative spirit world.

C.40 I have also stated that the giants became perverts because there were no female giants. Why did that happen? This happened because it was disobedience for the Fallen angels who are eternal beings and spiritual to have sex with physical women and something went wrong when they had sex with the women so that the masculine seed of the fallen angels was too dominant for the feminine egg cells in the human women.

C.41 After the Great Flood the giants sought for ways to come back into the physical plane and according to the *Hebrew Book of Jubilees* that is when sickness started on the earth.

C.42 The demons hated the Holy Spirit Mother as she is the one having to do with the creation of the females which they the giants were denied.

C.43 In the case of Satan himself why did he hate the Holy Spirit Mother and in fact the feminine side?

C.44 Satan is the height of arrogance and pride and hates for anyone telling him what is right and wrong. The Holy Spirit reflects God the father and embraces His laws of Light.

C.45 Satan has a Father and a Mother. As I have mentioned many times in this book that all Creation both in the physical world and the spiritual world are made up of male and female beings.

C.46 I have mentioned how on earth we all go through many different stages in life from baby to toddler to small child to child to teen to older teen to young adult to adult to middle aged to old and aged.

C.47 My question is how many of these stages do those born in the spirit world go through.? What about school age. I would like to suggest that in the case of Lucifer that although he was created as a perfect being with instruments embodied in him when he became an adult he chose to become proud and not honour His Holy Spirit Mother and her teachings of being submitted to both God and her teachings.

Ezekiel 28.13-14

[13] Thou hast been *in Eden the garden of God*; every precious stone was thy covering, the sardius, topaz, and the diamond, the beryl, the onyx, and the jasper, the sapphire, the emerald, and the carbuncle, and gold: the workmanship of thy tabrets and of thy pipes was prepared in thee in the day that thou wast created.

[14] Thou art the anointed cherub that covers; and I have set thee so: thou was upon the holy mountain of God; thou hast walked up and down in the midst of the stones of fire.

C.48 Satan rebelled when he declared that he would be as the Most High and would put his throned above the throne of God the Father. God immediately cast him down along with all of his angels. Lucifer then became Satan incarnate.

Isaiah 14.12-15

[12] How art thou fallen from heaven, O Lucifer, son of the morning! how art thou cut down to the ground, which didst weaken the nations!

[13] For thou hast said in thine heart, I will ascend into heaven, I will exalt my throne above the stars of God: I will sit also upon the mount of the congregation, in the sides of the north:

[14] I will ascend above the heights of the clouds; I will be like the most High.

[15] Yet thou shalt be brought down to hell, to the sides of the pit.

C.49 The Holy Spirit Mother obviously totally agreed with this decision by God the Father.

C.50 In the Book of Enoch it shows the first Fallen angels asking Enoch to plead with God the Father for them to get forgiveness and yet God said a resounding No! Why because they had done far to much damage and as a caught naughty boy they were not really sorry.

C.51 Satan and the Fallen angels mistake was to believe that both God the Father and God the Mother were mere pushovers and they have found out the hard way that they are wrong. God the Father and God the Mother are in fact strong disciplinarians with those who have gone astray like Satan.

C.52 In the case of Satan who started off good as a child and was probably close to his Mother the Holy Spirit at one time. He became very resentful and hateful against her and the feminine because She agreed with God the Father to throw Satan out of heaven for good. Satan is the backslider of backsliders. A real hateful bastard.

C.53 UNIVERSAL RECONCILIATION: In the 2nd *Book of Enoch,* it seems to mention that one day Satan and the Fallen angels (as they are eternal beings) will be forceable corrected and altered and will eventually get forgiven after being severely disciplined in the Lake of Fire unless of course they have the sense to truly repent before the time. Here is a verse from the Bible about this:

Revelation 20:10 - And the devil that deceived them was cast into the lake of fire and brimstone, where the beast and the false prophet are, and shall be tormented day and night for ever and ever.

C.54 Here are some of the verses mentioned about *Satan or Lucifer* as he was originally called which means a 'Being of Light' so sad that he in fact became a 'Being of Darkness' or the one in charge of the Darkness.

Book of Ezekiel Chapter 28.11-19

¹¹ Moreover the word of the Lord came unto me, saying,

¹² Son of man, take up a lamentation upon the king of Tyrus (Satan), and say unto him, Thus saith the Lord God; Thou seal up the sum, full of wisdom, and perfect in beauty.

¹³ Thou hast been *in Eden the garden of God*; every precious stone was thy covering, the sardius, topaz, and the diamond, the beryl, the onyx, and the jasper, the sapphire, the emerald, and the carbuncle, and gold: the workmanship of thy tabrets and of thy pipes was prepared in thee in the day that thou wast created.

¹⁴ Thou art the anointed cherub that covers; and I have set thee so: thou was upon the holy mountain of God; thou hast walked up and down in the midst of the stones of fire.

¹⁵ Thou was perfect in thy ways from the day that thou was created, till iniquity was found in thee.

¹⁶ By the multitude of thy merchandise they have filled the midst of thee with violence, and thou hast sinned: therefore I will cast thee as profane out of the mountain of God: and I will destroy thee, O covering cherub, from the midst of the stones of fire.

¹⁷ Thine heart was lifted up because of thy beauty, thou hast corrupted thy wisdom by reason of thy brightness: I will cast thee to the ground, I will lay thee before kings, that they may behold thee.

¹⁸ Thou hast defiled thy sanctuaries by the multitude of thine iniquities, by the iniquity of thy traffick; therefore will I bring forth a fire from the midst of thee, it shall devour thee, and I will bring thee to ashes upon the earth in the sight of all them that behold thee.

¹⁹ All they that know thee among the people shall be astonished at thee: thou shalt be a terror, and never shalt thou be any more.

ISAIAH CHAPTER 14 9-20

⁹ Hell from beneath is moved for thee to meet thee at thy coming: it stirreth up the dead for thee, even all the chief ones of the earth; it hath raised up from their thrones all the kings of the nations.

¹⁰ All they shall speak and say unto thee, Art thou also become weak as we? art thou become like unto us?

¹¹ Thy pomp is brought down to the grave, and the noise of thy viols: the worm is spread under thee, and the worms cover thee.

¹² How art thou fallen from heaven, O Lucifer, son of the morning! how art thou cut down to the ground, which didst weaken the nations!

¹³ For thou hast said in thine heart, I will ascend into heaven, I will exalt my throne above the stars of God: I will sit also upon the mount of the congregation, in the sides

of the north:

[14] I will ascend above the heights of the clouds; I will be like the most High.

[15] Yet thou shalt be brought down to hell, to the sides of the pit.

[16] They that see thee shall narrowly look upon thee, and consider thee, saying, Is this the man that made the earth to tremble, that did shake kingdoms;

[17] That made the world as a wilderness, and destroyed the cities thereof; that opened not the house of his prisoners?

[18] All the kings of the nations, even all of them, lie in glory, every one in his own house.

[19] But thou art cast out of thy grave like an abominable branch, and as the raiment of those that are slain, thrust through with a sword, that go down to the stones of the pit; as a carcase trodden under feet.

[20] Thou shalt not be joined with them in burial, because thou hast destroyed thy land, and slain thy people: the seed of evildoers shall never be renowned.

CHAPTER 26: LOVE

C.1 'Well, firstly you have to understand the power and place that love has in our universe. Love, you must realize, is the most powerful force that there is. Love is the very essence of God. It is the foundation on which all things were built and continue to exist. Without love, all that is would not be. Love is the foundation of everything, and it is the only thing that keeps the world alive and going. Love has creative powers. Jesus came to show the world His Father's love.

C.2 *Satan rejects love*, because real love is too invasive, too intrusive and revealing. It is too open when anyone has things to hide, and for that reason Satan hated and rejected Jesus.

C.3 But even death could not quell Jesus' love. He rose a victor over the forces opposed to love. All His miracles were done in love, His disciples were won in love, and His commandment to them was to 'love one another.' So whatever is done in love, God's love can never be wrong in the eyes of God. The Devil hates all that is love and does what he can to twist and destroy the pure impulse of God that love produces.' (Source: From the book about Hell: 'Journey to Gragau' a very insightful book by A.W.Trenholm- Available at Amazon.com

THE DANGERS OF RELATIONSHIPS WITH FALLEN ANGELS MASQUERADING AS ANGELS OF LIGHT

C.4 My book '*Enoch Insights*' talks about the *Fall of the Angels* and how they took unto them wives of all they chose.

I would like to elaborate on this topic, as many have suggested that there has to be more to the Story of Adam and Eve and Satan as the serpent in the Garden of Eden, than what is briefly mentioned in the Bible.

From the Book of Enoch, we also get the impression that *only male angels fell*, but is that the whole picture?

I would like to point out the real danger of the Angels as in regard to human women, in the beginning it was their beauty! Not just the beauty of the human women, but the beauty of the angels themselves!

The 'Watcher' angels were not supposed to materialize physically & to be seen by the women, at will.

EZE.27:3 And say unto Tyrus, 'O thou that art situate at the entry of the sea, which art a merchant of the people for many isles, Thus says the Lord GOD; 'O Tyrus, thou hast said, *'I am of perfect beauty'*.

C.5 As you know that I have already written in this book, that I believe that Cain was fathered by Satan, the deceiver who deceived Eve, once she had already fallen; having eaten of the apple' from the 'tree of the Knowledge of Good and Evil' and was already living in disobedience.

C.6 In the time of Jared around 500 years after Creation, the first 200 angels fell and came down on Mount Hermon. Later in time millions of angels eventually also fell. The Bible tells us in Revelations 12, that one third of God's

Angels eventually fell. It is stated that they didn't all fall at once, but that many of them were seduced! By whom?

C.7 In **Enoch chapter 8.1-2** 'And Azazel taught men to make swords and knives, and shields, and breastplates, and made known to them the metals of the earth and the art of working with them, and bracelets, and ornaments, and the use of antimony, and the beautifying of the eyelids, and all kinds of costly stones, and all colouring tinctures.' And there arose much godlessness, and they committed fornication, and they were led astray, and became corrupt in all their ways.

C.8 Women were taught how to beautiful themselves, and to be experts at seducing both men and angels.

Initially, the first 200 Fallen angels seduced the women on earth, later with the knowledge of how to be seductive, it would seem that the *human women seduced millions of angels*. Why would they be tempted to do exactly that? Why would angels of God fall for them?

C.9 Why is it that most people don't get to see angels? It would seem that God has put a barrier in the spirit against *too much fraternization* between the spirit world and the physical world, because of the problems mentioned, that all started before the Great Flood.

C.10 I notice that in Gothic art there are many pictures of female 'Fallen Angels'. Is there actually any evidence for this? If the male original 'Fallen angels' were irresistible to the beautiful women on earth, *imagine how much more dangerously seductive women from the spirit world would be to men on earth?* Not a good idea! It would be very distracting! For these reasons, I believe that God has made a barrier between the physical realm and the spiritual. It was probably very different before the Great Flood. That is not to say that sexual union doesn't still happen between 'Fallen angels' and women on the earth, but it is not normally so visible as in the Pre-Flood times. In modern times, people talk about being abducted by 'Aliens and being sexually abused', but it is the same old thing as before the great Flood, just in a slightly different manner.

C.11 THE DANGERS OF VANITY FOR WOMEN!

I think that it is a big temptation for women to want to be something higher than human, especially if their mate/partner is not the most spiritual of persons. Why is it that 80% of those who go into Gothic Art and even into witchcraft are all women?

C.12 Is it because they desire the higher powers afforded by the Fallen Angels, without necessarily realizing what they are getting into? Why do women spend hours and hours dolling themselves up to look amazingly beautiful? Is it really to attract just their mate or boyfriend if they have one? Or is there in the case of certain very shallow women a much deeper reason? Women say they do it because they want to be noticed. Understood! Everyone wants to be seen as nice and beautiful, if at all possible, but I think that there can also be a big danger here for women, if they over-do on this beautifying of themselves, just like the original women on the earth before the

Great Flood. *Important not to attract the wrong kind of people or worse yet evil entities.*

CHAPTER 27: GENESIS

Genesis Chapter 1

² "And the earth was without form, and void; and darkness *was* upon the face of the deep. And the *Spirit of God* moved upon the face of the waters.

C.1 The big question is whose spirit is this talking about? It says the *Spirit of God* and most people assume that it is talking about *God the Father* due to them believing in the *all masculine Trinity* but apparently it is talking about the *Holy Spirit* which turns out to be *feminine* and is in fact the *Holy Spirit Mother* not the Father. *She* is the *wife of God*.

C.2 Did you know that the ancient Hebrews knew that the Spirit of God mentioned in this verse was Mother God?

C.3 Why has someone deliberately altered the scriptures in the past to deny the female side of the godhead giving an all-male Trinity? Why is this fact so important? Because it makes all the difference in the world to know that *male* and *female* is not just a fleshly attribute but that the whole of God's Creation both physical and in fact the entire spirit world are all *male and female* and that is the basis of Creation itself.

C.4 Without male and female there is no creation. All because there is a female Goddess in the Trinity.

C.5 Look what it says when God created the physical world as He appears to be talking with a female in the description of the verse. What female? The only one that was around before Creation God's wife the Holy Spirit Mother.

²⁶ And God said, 'Let us make man in **our** image', after our likeness: and let them have dominion over the fish of the sea, and over the fowl of the air, and over the cattle, and over all the earth, and over every creeping thing that creeps upon the earth.

²⁷ So God created man in his own image, in the image of God created he him; *male and female* created he them.

C.6 These last 2 Bible verses prove that God was talking with a *fellow Creator* who was *female* as they created both *male and female*. God said let *us* create man in our image and *male and female* created He them.

Genesis Chapter 2.7

⁷ And the Lord God formed man of the dust of the ground and breathed into his nostrils the *breath of life*; and man became a living soul.

C.7 *'Breath of Life'* is another name for *Holy Spirit Mother*. She is the mother of all things created.

Genesis Chapter 3.20

²⁰ And Adam called his wife's name Eve; because she was the *mother* of all living.

C.8 This verse clearly shows that Eve was the *mother of all living* and that it was her responsibility to bring forth children in order for the human race to continue. The problem we have in the West today is that most woman are not having babies anymore but prefer not to have children which is causing the population to go down and the latest stats show that the white races are disappearing fast.

C.9 It is now stated that unless all women start having an average of 3 children each then the population of the planet is going to go down drastically and quickly which is by design of the 'controllers'.

C.10 Satan wants to destroy all of God's Creation and unfortunately at the present time he is largely succeeding.

1) He is destroying the atmosphere with chemtrails and other poisonous chemicals. 2) The latest is that governments are admitting they want to blot out the sun

3) The seas are already heavily polluted

4) The earth itself has been heavily polluted by industry

5) The people have been deliberately poisoned by big pharma and their drugs

6) The list goes on and on...

C.11 Fortunately for us God will very soon put an end to Satan and all the evil destruction.

Isaiah 2:19 And they shall go into the holes of the rocks, and into the caves of the earth, for fear of the LORD, and for the glory of his majesty, when he arises to shake terribly the earth.

Revelation 20:10 And the devil that deceived them was cast into the lake of fire and brimstone, where the beast and the false prophet are, and shall be tormented day and night for ever and ever.

Genesis Chapter 5.1

¹This is the book of the generations of Adam. In the day that God *created man, in the likeness of God* made he him;

C.12 It is essential to know that there is God the Father and God the Mother as well as God the Son. They are a family, which the next verse makes so clear.

² Male and female created he them; and blessed them, and called their name Adam, in the day when they were created.

C.13 Why were Adam and Eve made male and female? Because they were created in the form of *Father God* and *Mother God*. Plain and simple. It was a tragic day when that knowledge was taken away and changed to 'The Lord our God is one God' by the Jews. When you check the original Hebrew you find the word for God *Elohim* which is in the plural form (*Elohim* then came to be used so frequently in reference to specific deities, both male and female Elohim - Wikipedia),

Genesis Chapter 6.1-3

[1] And it came to pass, when men began to multiply on the face of the earth, and daughters were born unto them,

[2] That the *sons of God* saw the daughters of men that they were fair; and they took them wives of all which they chose.

C.14 The sons of God were the angels that fell or better know as the Fallen Angels.

[3] And the Lord said, *My spirit* shall not always strive with man, for that he also is flesh: yet his days shall be *an hundred and twenty years*.

C.15 *My Spirit* will not always strive with man. The Holy Spirit Mother was always telling mankind to be loving and kind and not to be violent and destructive. She must have warned mankind to stay away from the Fallen angels. This reminds me of a verse in the Book of Enoch.

C.16 *God's Spirit* is also known as *Wisdom* in the Old Testament Bible in the Proverbs and also in the *Book of Enoch*.

BOOK OF ENOCH CHAPTER 42.1-3.

1. **Wisdom** found no place where she might dwell;

Then a dwelling-place was assigned her in the heavens.

2. **Wisdom** went forth to make her dwelling among the children of men,

And found no dwelling-place:

3. **Wisdom** returned to her place,

And took her seat among the angels.

C.17 In the *Book of Enoch chapter 42* there is also another spirit mentioned which is the exact opposite of the *Holy Spirit Mother* an evil feminine spirit of *Unrighteousness*.

BOOK OF ENOCH 42.3

And *unrighteousness* went forth from her chambers:

Whom she sought not she found,

And dwelt with them,

As rain in a desert

And dew on a thirsty land.

GENESIS CHAPTER 6.4-6

[4] There were *giants* in the earth in those days; and also after that, when the *sons of*

God came in unto the daughters of men, and they bare children to them, the same became *mighty men* which were of old, *men of renown.*

⁵ And God saw that the wickedness of man was great in the earth, and that every imagination of the thoughts of his heart was only *evil* continually.

⁶ And it repented the LORD that he had made man on the earth, and it *grieved him at his heart.*

C.18 When it says it repented the *Lord* that he had made man on the earth and it *grieved* him at this heart it should really state it *grieved them* (*Father Mother and Son* as they are all *Creators*) in Hebrew Elohim(plural) meaning Gods.

C.19 Of course since the truth is that there is God and the Father and God the Mother it obviously grieved the Holy Spirit Mother as well in what was going on the earth in Pre-Flood times. Scripture states 'For these three are One and agree in One.'

1 John 5.7' For there are three that bear record in heaven, the Father, the Word, and the Holy Ghost: and these three are one.

C.20 Evil descended by the Fallen Angels, but it was started in the Garden of Eden by Satan disguised in a snake.

GENESIS CHAPTER 6 7-8,12-15,17-22

⁷ And the Lord said, I will *destroy man* whom I have created from the face of the earth; both man, and beast, and the creeping thing, and the fowls of the air; for it *repenteth me that I have made them.*

⁸ But Noah found *grace* in the eyes of the Lord.

¹² And God looked upon the earth, and, behold, it was corrupt; for *all flesh had corrupted his way upon the earth.*

¹³ And God said unto Noah, The end of all flesh is come before me; for the earth is filled with violence through them; and, behold, I will destroy them with the earth.

¹⁴ Make thee an ark of gopher wood; rooms shalt thou make in the ark, and shalt pitch it within and without with pitch.

¹⁵ And this is the fashion which thou shalt make it of: The length of the ark shall be three hundred cubits, the breadth of it fifty cubits, and the height of it thirty cubits.

¹⁷ And, behold, I, even I, do bring a flood of waters upon the earth, to destroy all flesh, wherein is the breath of life, from under heaven; and every thing that is in the earth shall die.

C.21 *Breath of life* is an expression which means that life given by the *Holy Spirit Mother.* The Holy Spirit Mother is the mother of all life.

¹⁸ But with thee will I *establish my covenant*; and thou shalt come into the ark, thou,

and thy sons, and thy wife, and thy sons' wives with thee.

[19] And of every living thing of all flesh, two of every sort shalt thou bring into the ark, to keep them alive with thee; they shall be *male and female*.

C.22 Notice how many times God mentions (or I should say emphasizes) the importance of *male and female*. It does not say any other strange combinations. Why because God wants unions that could become *fruitful and multiply*. It does not say chimeras or giants or any other strange possibilities but simply that which is natural male and female. There is something almost magical to the union of male and female. Something heavenly. Something that is more than creative.

[20] Of fowls after their kind, and of cattle after their kind, of every creeping thing of the earth after his kind, *two of every sort* shall come unto thee, to keep them alive.

[21] And take thou unto thee of all food that is eaten, and thou shalt gather it to thee; and it shall be for food for thee, and for them.

[22] Thus did Noah; according to all that *God commanded him, so did he*.

GENESIS CHAPTER 7.9,11,13-17,20-22

[9] There went in *two and two* unto Noah into the ark, the *male and the female*, as God had commanded Noah.

[11] In the six hundredth year of Noah's life, in the second month, the seventeenth day of the month, the same day were all the fountains of the great deep broken up, and the windows of heaven were opened. [12] And the rain was upon the earth forty days and forty nights.

[13] In the selfsame (same) day entered Noah, and Shem, and Ham, and Japheth, the sons of Noah, and Noah's wife, and the three wives of his sons with them, into the ark;

[14] They, and every beast after his kind, and all the cattle after their kind, and every creeping thing that creepeth upon the earth after his kind, and every fowl after his kind, every bird of every sort.

[15] And they went in unto Noah into the ark, *two and two* of all flesh, wherein is the *breath of life*.

[16] And they that went in, went in *male and female* of all flesh, as God had commanded him: and the Lord shut him in.

[17] And the flood was *forty days* upon the earth; and the waters increased, and bare up the ark, and it was lift up above the earth.

[19] And the waters prevailed exceedingly upon the earth; and all the high hills, that were under the whole heaven, were covered.

[20] **Fifteen cubits upward** did the waters prevail; and the **mountains were covered.**

[21] And all flesh died that moved upon the earth, both of fowl, and of cattle, and of beast, and of every creeping thing that creepeth upon the earth, and every man:

[22] All in whose nostrils was the breath of life, of all that was in the dry land, died. [23] And every living substance was destroyed which was upon the face of the ground, both man, and cattle, and the creeping things, and the fowl of the heaven; and they were destroyed from the earth: and Noah only remained alive, and they that were with him in the ark.

[24] And the waters prevailed upon the earth an hundred and fifty days. And God remembered Noah, and every living thing, and all the cattle that was with him in the ark: and God made a wind to pass over the earth, and the waters assuaged;

GENESIS CHAPTER 8.1-12,16-20

[1] And God remembered Noah, and every living thing, and all the cattle that was with him in the ark: and God made a wind to pass over the earth, and the waters assuaged;

[2] The fountains also of the deep and the windows of heaven were stopped, and the rain from heaven was restrained;

C.23 These are very interesting expressions 1) Fountains of the 2) Deep. What is that talking about? Well, water was both coming down from the sky, but it was also bubbling up from under the oceans as a much a bigger supply of waters was coming up from the 'underground seas', which were also under the land as well as the seas. This can be best understood if one realizes that the earth is actually hollow and not solid. The crust of the earth being around 300 to 500 miles thick. Contained in the crust are vast reservoirs of water or underground seas. It was these seas apparently that were the basis for the 'Fountains of the Deep' expression.

[3] And the waters returned from off the earth continually: and after the end of the hundred and fifty days the waters were abated.

[4] And the ark rested in the seventh month, on the seventeenth day of the month, upon the mountains of Ararat.

[5] And the waters decreased continually until the tenth month: in the tenth month, on the first day of the month, were the tops of the mountains seen.

[6] And it came to pass at the end of forty days, that Noah opened the window of the ark which he had made:

[7] And he sent forth a raven, which went forth to and fro, until the waters were dried up from off the earth.

[8] Also he sent forth a *dove* from him, to see if the waters were abated from off the face of the ground;

⁹ But the dove found no rest for the sole of her foot, and she returned unto him into the ark, for the waters were on the face of the whole earth: then he put forth his hand, and took her, and pulled her in unto him into the ark.

¹⁰ And he stayed yet other seven days; and again he sent forth the dove out of the ark;

¹¹ And the dove came in to him in the evening; and, lo, in her mouth was an *olive leaf* plucked off: so Noah knew that the waters were abated from off the earth.

¹² And he stayed yet other seven days; and sent forth the dove; which returned not again unto him anymore.

¹⁵ And God spake unto Noah, saying,

¹⁶ Go forth of the ark, thou, and thy wife, and thy sons, and thy sons' wives with thee.

¹⁷ Bring forth with thee every living thing that is with thee, of all flesh, both of fowl, and of cattle, and of every creeping thing that creeps upon the earth; that they may breed abundantly in the earth, and be fruitful, and multiply upon the earth.

¹⁸ And Noah went forth, and his sons, and his wife, and his sons' wives with him:

¹⁹ Every beast, every creeping thing, and every fowl, and whatsoever creeps upon the earth, after their kinds, went forth out of the ark.

²⁰ And Noah built an *altar* unto the Lord; and took of every clean beast, and of every clean fowl, and offered burnt offerings on the altar.

GENESIS CHAPTER 9.1-9,11-17

¹ And God blessed Noah and his sons, and said unto them, '*Be fruitful, and multiply*', *and replenish the earth.*

² And the fear of you and the dread of you shall be upon every beast of the earth, and upon every fowl of the air, upon all that moveth upon the earth, and upon all the fishes of the sea; into your hand are they delivered.

³ Every moving thing that lives shall be meat for you; even as the green herb have I given you all things.

C.24 Before the Great Flood mankind did not eat meat but only vegetables. After the Great Flood of Noah's time mankind were required to eat meat as the conditions on the earth had changed and mankind need the meat fro greater strength as mankind who used to live to be over 900 years now only lived to be 120 years then eventually much lower.

⁴ But flesh with the life thereof, which is the blood thereof, shall ye not eat.

⁵ And surely your blood of your lives will I require; at the hand of every beast will I require it, and at the hand of man; at the hand of every man's brother will I require the life of man.

⁶ Whoso sheds man's blood, by man shall his blood be shed: for in the image of God made he man.

⁷ And you, be ye *fruitful*, and *multiply*; bring forth *abundantly* in the earth, and multiply therein.

⁸ And God spake unto Noah, and to his sons with him, saying,

⁹ And I, behold, I establish my covenant with you, and with your seed after you;

¹¹ And I will establish my covenant with you, neither shall all flesh be cut off any more by the waters of a flood; neither shall there any more be a flood to destroy the earth.

¹² And God said, This is the token of the covenant which I make between me and you and every living creature that is with you, for perpetual generations:

¹³ I do set *my bow in the cloud*, and it shall be for a token of a covenant between me and the earth.

C.25 RAINBOW The colours of which are supposed to represent God's covenant with mankind that he would never flood the earth again. At least not with water. Next time it will be with fire.

Revelation 4.3 "And he that sat was to look upon like a jasper and a sardine stone: and *there was* a *rainbow* round about the throne, in sight like unto an emerald."

¹⁴ And it shall come to pass, when I bring a cloud over the earth, that the bow shall be seen in the cloud:

¹⁵ And I will remember my covenant, which is between me and you and every living creature of all flesh; and the waters shall no more become a flood to destroy all flesh.

¹⁶ And the bow shall be in the cloud; and I will look upon it, that I may remember the *everlasting covenant* between God and every living creature of all flesh that is upon the earth.

¹⁷ And God said unto Noah, This is the token of the covenant, which I have established between me and all flesh that is upon the earth.

GENESIS CHAPTER 11.4-9

⁴ And they said, Go to, let us build us a city and a tower, whose top may reach unto heaven; and let us make us a name, lest we be scattered abroad upon the face of the whole earth.

⁵ And the LORD came down to see the city and the tower, which the children of men built.

⁶ And the LORD said, Behold, the people *is* one, and they have all one language; and this they begin to do: and now nothing will be restrained from them, which they have imagined to do.

⁷Go to, let us go down, and there confound their language, that they may not understand one another's speech.

⁸ So the Lord scattered them abroad from there over the face of all the earth, and they left off building the city.

⁹Therefore is the name of it called Babel;

C.26 *Babel* means *Confusion* of tongues or languages

CHAPTER 28: BOOK OF ACTS -key verses

Introduction: I have taken the most important verses from the Book of Acts which mention the *Holy Ghost* or miracles or angels as well as visions, dreams or angelic intervention. I have mentioned situations of tremendous witness about Jesus.

I think that it is truly inspiring and wonderful how the verses of Joel were indeed fulfilled in the anointing of the *Holy Ghost* in the New Testament times.

In Old Testament times God anointed one particular man or woman of God upon occasion such as Enoch, Noah, Abraham. Isaac, Jacob and the 12 Patriarchs, Moses, David, Esther, and all the prophets for a season but it was usually only one or two persons in a given time period.

However, the marvel of the New Testament Book of Acts was how God raised up so many on fire witnesses for the Kingdom of God.

It was as if Jesus had to die first as the Messiah for the salvation of mankind before the full power of the Holy Spirit could be fully realized upon the earth to pour forth and greatly multiply the witness of Salvation. The Old Testament predicted that the Messiah would come and save the whole world from the influence of both Satan and the sins of mankind.

ACTS Chapter 1

1 The former treatise have I made, O Theophilus of all that Jesus began both to do and teach,

2 Until the day in which he was taken up, after that he through the Holy Ghost had given commandments unto the apostles whom he had chosen:

C.1 'That Jesus began both to do and teach', 'until the day in which he was taken up' -that is the time exact time period when He sent His commandments to the apostles through His Holy Spirit Mother.

C.2 After Jesus had gone to Heaven the *Holy Ghost* or in other words the Holy Spirit Mother was His ambassador to his disciples, exactly as he had predicted would happen.

C.3 In the original language this was what *John 16.7* actually said:

John 16:7 Nevertheless I tell you the truth; It is expedient for you that I go away: for if I go not away, the *Comforter* will not come unto you; but if I depart, I will send *Her* unto you.

C.4 Jesus had also stated that *She* was the *Comforter* which indeed tends to be a feminine role.

John 14.26

[26] But the Comforter, which is the Holy Ghost, whom the Father will send in my name, *she* shall teach you all things, and bring all things to your remembrance, whatsoever I have said unto you.

Acts 1.3 To whom also he shewed himself alive after his *passion* by many infallible proofs, being seen of them forty days, and speaking of the things pertaining to the *kingdom of God*:

C.5 It is true that Jesus was seen of the disciples upon many occasions right after His resurrection.

Matthew 28.9 And as they went to tell his disciples, behold, Jesus met them, saying, All hail. And they came and held him by the feet and worshipped him.

C.6 The Book of Joel predicted that God's Spirit would be poured out abundantly, which happened after the Resurrection of the Messiah Jesus Christ.

Joel 2.28 "And it shall come to pass afterward, *that* I will pour out my spirit upon all flesh; and your sons and your daughters shall prophesy, your old men shall dream dreams, your young maidens shall see visions:"

Acts 2.17-18

And it shall come to pass in the last days, saith God, I will pour out of my Spirit upon all flesh: and your sons and your daughters shall prophesy, and your young men shall see visions, and your old men shall dream dreams.

Acts 2.33 Therefore being by the right hand of God exalted, and having received of the Father the promise of the *Holy Ghost*, he hath shed forth this, which ye now see and hear.

Acts 2.38 Then Peter said unto them, Repent, and be baptized every one of you in the name of Jesus Christ for the remission of sins, and ye shall receive the gift of the *Holy Ghost*.

But those things, which God before had shewed by the mouth of all his prophets, that Christ should suffer, he hath so fulfilled.

Acts 3.20-22

20 And he shall send Jesus Christ, which before was preached unto you:

21 Whom the heaven must receive until the times of restitution of all things, which God hath spoken by the mouth of all his holy prophets since the world began.

22 "For Moses truly said unto the fathers, A prophet shall the Lord your God raise up unto you of your brethren, like unto me; him shall ye hear in all things whatsoever he shall say.

Acts 4.12 "Neither is there salvation in any other: for there is none other name under heaven given among men, whereby we must be saved (Jesus)."

Acts 4.13 Now when they saw the boldness of Peter and John, and perceived that they were unlearned and ignorant men, they marvelled; and they took knowledge of them, that they had been with Jesus.

Acts 4.19-20 But Peter and John answered and said unto them, Whether it be right in the sight of God to hearken unto you more than unto God, judge ye. For we cannot but speak the things which we have seen and heard.

Acts 4.32-35 And when they had prayed, the place was shaken where they were assembled together; and they were all filled with the *Holy Ghost*, and they spake the word of God with boldness.

[32] And the multitude of them that believed were of one heart and of one soul: neither said any of them that ought of the things which he possessed was his own; but they had all things common.

[33] And with *great power* gave the apostles witness of the resurrection of the Lord Jesus: and great grace was upon them all.

[34] Neither was there any among them that lacked: for as many as were possessors of lands or houses sold them, and brought the prices of the things that were sold,

[35] And laid them down at the apostles' feet: and distribution was made unto every man according as he had need.

Acts 5.19-20,29

[19] But the *angel* of the Lord by night opened the prison doors, and brought them forth, and said,

[20] Go, stand and speak in the temple to the people all the *words of this life*.

[29] Then Peter and the other apostles answered and said, We ought to obey God rather than men.

Acts 5.32 And we are his witnesses of these things; and so is also the *Holy Ghost*, whom God hath given to them that obey him.

Acts 6.3-4

[3] Therefore, brethren, look ye out among you seven men of honest report, full of the *Holy Ghost and wisdom,* whom we may appoint over this business.

[4] But we will give ourselves continually to prayer, and to the ministry of the word.

[15] And all that sat in the council, looking steadfastly on him, saw his face as it had been the face of an angel.

Acts 7.47-53,55-56

[47] But Solomon built him an house.

[48] Howbeit the most High dwelleth not in temples made with hands; as saith the prophet,

[49] Heaven is my throne, and earth is my footstool: what house will ye build me? saith

the Lord: or what is the place of my rest?

⁵⁰ Hath not my hand made all these things?

⁵¹ Ye stiff-necked and uncircumcised in heart and ears, ye do always resist the *Holy Ghost*: as your fathers did, so do ye.

⁵² Which of the prophets have not your fathers persecuted? and they have slain them which shewed before of the coming of the Just One; of whom ye have been now the betrayers and murderers:

⁵³ Who have received the law by the disposition of angels and have not kept it.

C.7 This is a very revealing verse how that the religious people of the Pharisees and Sadducees had not been given the laws by God by Satan and his Fallen angels. They had the letter of the law but not the Spirit of God. The Holy Spirit Mother they did not have guiding them, but Satan.

⁵⁵ But he, being full of the *Holy Ghost*, looked up steadfastly into heaven, and saw the glory of God, and Jesus standing on the right hand of God,

⁵⁶ And said, Behold, I see the heavens opened, and the Son of man standing on the right hand of God.

Acts 8.12,14-17

¹² But when they believed Philip preaching the things concerning the kingdom of God, and the name of Jesus Christ, they were baptized, both men and women.

¹⁴ Now when the apostles which were at Jerusalem heard that Samaria had received the word of God, they sent unto them Peter and John:

¹⁵ Who, when they were come down, prayed for them, that they might receive the *Holy Ghost:*

¹⁶ (For as yet she was fallen upon none of them: only they were baptized in the name of the Lord Jesus.)

¹⁷ Then laid they their hands on them, and they received the *Holy Ghost*.

Acts 8.26,29-31,39-40

²⁶ And the **angel** of the Lord spake unto Philip, saying, Arise, and go toward the south unto the way that goeth down from Jerusalem unto Gaza, which is desert.

²⁹ Then the *Spirit (Holy Spirit Mother)* said unto Philip, Go near, and join thyself to this chariot.

³⁰ And Philip ran thither to him, and heard him read the prophet Esaias, and said, Understand thou what thou read?

³¹ And he said, How can I, except some man should guide me? And he desired Philip

that he would come up and sit with him.

ⁿ³⁹ And when they were come up out of the water, *the Spirit of the Lord (Holy Spirit Mother)* caught away Philip, that the eunuch saw him no more: and he went on his way rejoicing.

C.8 Here is a good example in the following verse how Jesus and His *Holy Spirit Mother* work together side by side.

1.John 5.7 "For there are three that bear record in heaven, the Father, the Word, and the *Holy Ghost:* and these three are one."

⁴⁰ But Philip was found at Azotus: and passing through he preached in all the cities, till he came to Caesarea.

C.9 Azotus was 200 miles away!

Acts 9.17-18,27,31

¹⁷ And Ananias went his way and entered the house; and laying his hands on him he said, "Brother Saul, the Lord [a]Jesus, who appeared to you on the road as you came, has sent me that you may receive your sight and be filled with the *Holy Spirit.*"

¹⁸ Immediately there fell from his eyes *something* like scales, and he received his sight at once; and he arose and was baptized.

²⁷ But Barnabas took him and brought him to the apostles. He told them how Saul on his journey had seen the Lord and that the Lord had spoken to him, and how in Damascus he had preached fearlessly in the name of Jesus.

³¹ Then had the churches rest throughout all Judaea and Galilee and Samaria, and were edified; and walking in the fear of the Lord, and in the 'comfort' of the Holy Ghost, were multiplied.

C.10 Holy Spirit Mother had great delight in the disciples

Acts 10.3,11,19,44-45-47

³ He saw in a *vision* evidently about the ninth hour of the day an *angel of God* coming in to him, and saying unto him, Cornelius.

Acts 11.21,24-26,28

²¹ And the hand of the Lord was with them: and a great number believed and turned unto the Lord.

²⁴ For he was a good man, and full of the **Holy Ghost** and of faith: and much people was added unto the Lord.

C.11 Here it shows that God could even talk to a government official and tell him the truth by visions.

²⁵ Then departed Barnabas to Tarsus, for to seek Saul:

²⁶ And when he had found him, he brought him unto Antioch. And it came to pass, that a whole year they assembled themselves with the church, and taught much people. And the disciples were called *Christians* first in Antioch.

C.12 Christian means follower of Christ and his teachings of the Word of God.

²⁸ And there stood up one of them named Agabus, and signified *by the Spirit* that there should be great dearth throughout all the world: which came to pass in the days of Claudius Caesar. ⁷ And, behold, the *angel of the Lord* came upon him, and a light shined in the prison: and he smote Peter on the side, and raised him up, saying, Arise up quickly. And his chains fell off from his hands.

C.13 Dearth = great famine

Acts 12.8-10,23

⁸ And the *angel* said unto him, Gird thyself, and bind on thy sandals. And so he did. And he saith unto him, Cast thy garment about thee, and follow me.

⁹ And he went out, and followed him; and wist not that it was true which was done by the angel; but thought he saw a *vision*.

C.14 Wist not = knew not

¹⁰ When they were past the first and the second ward, they came unto the iron gate that leadeth unto the city; which opened to them of his own accord: and they went out, and passed on through one street; and forthwith the angel departed from him.

C.15 Look what happened to Herod the king. He had just murdered James the apostle and then given an arrogant speech for which the people praised him as a god and then the judgement of God fell upon him.

²³ And immediately the *angel* of the Lord smote him, because he gave not God the glory: and he was eaten of worms and gave up the ghost.

Acts 13.2,4,10-11,52

² As they ministered to the Lord, and fasted, the *Holy Ghost* said, Separate me Barnabas and Saul for the work whereunto I have called them.

⁴ So they, being sent forth by the *Holy Ghost*, departed unto Seleucia; and from thence they sailed to Cyprus. ⁹ Then Saul, (who also is called Paul,) filled with the *Holy Ghost*, set his eyes on him.

¹⁰ And said, O full of all subtilty and all mischief, thou child of the devil, thou enemy of all righteousness, wilt thou not cease to pervert the right ways of the Lord?

C.16 Strong judgement meted out to a devil.

¹¹ And now, behold, the hand of the Lord is upon thee, and thou shalt be blind, not seeing the sun for a season. And immediately there fell on him a mist and a darkness; and he went about seeking some to lead him by the hand.

⁵² And the disciples were filled with joy, and with the *Holy Ghost*.

C.17 Look how the Holy Spirit Mother loved the disciples and filled them with joy. Such a beautiful verse of Heavenly love.

Acts 14.8-10

[8] And there sat a certain man at Lystra, impotent in his feet, being a cripple from his mother's womb, who never had walked:

[9] The same heard Paul speak: who steadfastly beholding him, and perceiving that he had faith to be healed,

Acts 16 6,9-10,15-15,24-32,40

[6] Now when they had gone throughout Phrygia and the region of Galatia, and were forbidden of the *Holy Ghost* to preach the word in Asia,.

C.18 Look how the Holy Ghost instructed the disciples of Christ as to what to do and what not to do and when was the best time to do it. On this particular occasion She actually told them not to go and preach the Gospel in Asia at that particular time.

[9] And a vision appeared to Paul in the night; There stood a man of Macedonia, and prayed him, saying, Come over into Macedonia, and help us.

[10] And after he had seen the *vision*, immediately we endeavoured to go into Macedonia, assuredly gathering that the Lord had called us for to preach the gospel unto them.

[14] And a certain woman named Lydia, a seller of purple, of the city of Thyatira, which worshipped God, heard us: whose heart the Lord opened, that she attended unto the things which were spoken of Paul.

[15] And when she was baptized, and her household, she besought us, saying, If ye have judged me to be faithful to the Lord, come into my house, and abide there. And she constrained us.

[24] Who, having received such a charge, thrust them into the inner prison, and made their feet fast in the stocks.

[25] And at midnight Paul and Silas prayed, and sang praises unto God: and the prisoners heard them.

[26] And suddenly there was a great earthquake, so that the foundations of the prison were shaken: and immediately all the doors were opened, and every one's bands were loosed.

Acts 18.1-2,9-10,25-26

[1] After these things Paul departed from Athens, and came to Corinth;

[2] And found a certain Jew named Aquila, born in Pontus, lately come from Italy, with his wife Priscilla; (because that Claudius had commanded all Jews to depart from

Rome:) and came unto them.

⁹ Then spake the Lord to Paul in the night by a *vision*, Be not afraid, but speak, and hold not thy peace:

¹⁰ For I am with thee, and no man shall set on thee to hurt thee: for I have much people in this city. ²⁴ And a certain Jew named Apollos, born at Alexandria, an eloquent man, and mighty in the scriptures, came to Ephesus.

²⁵ This man was instructed in the way of the Lord; and being fervent in the spirit, he spake and taught diligently the things of the Lord, knowing only the *baptism of John*.

²⁶ And he began to speak boldly in the synagogue: whom when Aquila and Priscilla had heard, they took him unto them, and expounded unto him the way of God more perfectly.

Acts 20.19-26,28,35

¹⁹ Serving the Lord with all humility of mind, and with many tears, and temptations, which befell me by the lying in wait of the Jews:

C.19 Paul was not some pompous bishop or pastor in an old church building going through a bunch of ancient ceremonies, but he was suffering a lot whilst he preached the Gospel every day with tears. He had enemies persecuting him all the time and yet he had the boldness from the Holy Spirit to keep telling everyone about Jesus every day.

C.20 Christianity used to be the followers or disciples not sitting in church buildings once a week for an hour doing nothing, but it was full-time forsaking all as Jesus had commanded his disciples in the Gospel of Luke.

Luke 14.33 So likewise whosoever he be of you that forsakes not all that he hath he cannot be my disciple

C.21 What does 'Forsaking all mean? It means giving up all the things of this world that are worldly and false and spending ones full time as a missionary *telling others about Salvation through Jesus Christ the Messiah*. Teaching others to read the word of God daily and not just a few verses in a church building on a Sunday. What a different world we are in today!

C.22 Just reading the *four Gospels* makes it very clear what a Christian and disciple of Christ is supposed to be like. A full-time worker for Christ and certainly not a loafer. Everyone can find something to do for Christ.

²⁰ And how I kept back nothing that was profitable unto you, but have shewed you, and have taught you publicly, and from house to house,

²¹ Testifying both to the Jews, and also to the Greeks, repentance toward God, and faith toward our Lord Jesus Christ.

²² And now, behold, I go bound in the spirit unto Jerusalem, not knowing the things that shall befall me there:

²³ Save that the *Holy Ghost* witnesseth in every city, saying that bonds and afflictions abide me.

²⁴ But none of these things move me, neither count I my life dear unto myself, so that I might finish my course with joy, and the ministry, which I have received of the Lord Jesus, to testify the *gospel* of the *grace of God*.

²⁵ And now, behold, I know that ye all, among whom I have gone preaching the kingdom of God, shall see my face no more.

²⁶ Wherefore I take you to record this day, that I am pure from the blood of all men.

²⁸ Take heed therefore unto yourselves, and to all the flock, over the which the *Holy Ghost* hath made you overseers, to feed the church of God, which he hath purchased with his own blood.

³⁵ I have shewed you all things, how that so labouring ye ought to support the weak, and to remember the words of the Lord Jesus, how he said, It is more blessed to give than to receive.

Acts 21.4,11-13-14

⁴ And finding disciples, we tarried there seven days: who said to Paul through *the Spirit*, that he should not go up to Jerusalem.

¹¹ And when he was come unto us, he took Paul's girdle, and bound his own hands and feet, and said, Thus saith the *Holy Ghost*, So shall the Jews at Jerusalem bind the man that owneth this girdle, and shall deliver him into the hands of the Gentiles.

C.23 The Holy Spirit as well as the disciples warned Paul not to return to Jerusalem otherwise he would be bound. One prophet even warned him telling him that he would end up dead if he retuned to Jerusalem, which unfortunately is what would happen. If Paul had listened to the Holy Spirit Mother and the disciples at that time maybe he would have lived longer to keep preaching the Gospel of Jesus Christ. I consider him to have been one of the greatest of the early Christians as in regard to how many people he reached with the Gospel. Praise the Lord.

¹² And when we heard these things, both we, and they of that place, besought him not to go up to Jerusalem.

¹³ Then Paul answered, What mean ye to weep and to break mine heart? for I am ready not to be bound only, but also to die at Jerusalem for the name of the Lord Jesus.

¹⁴ And when he would not be persuaded, we ceased, saying, The will of the Lord be done.

Acts 22.6-9,17 Paul gives his testimony after having returned to Jerusalem

⁶ And it came to pass, that, as I made my journey, and was come nigh unto Damascus

about noon, suddenly there *shone from heaven a great light* round about me.

⁷ And I fell unto the ground, and heard a voice saying unto me, Saul, Saul, why persecutest thou me?

⁸ And I answered, Who art thou, Lord? And he said unto me, I am Jesus of Nazareth, whom thou persecute.

⁹ And they that were with me saw indeed the light, and were afraid; but they heard not the voice of him that spake to me.

¹⁷ And it came to pass, that, when I was come again to Jerusalem, even while I prayed in the temple, I was in a *trance*.

C.24 What did Paul mean that he was in a trance. It simply means that after he had prayed desperately that he was taken into the spirit world to be shown what God wanted him to see whilst his companions did not see what he saw.

²⁰ And when the blood of thy martyr Stephen was shed, I also was standing by, and consenting unto his death, and kept the raiment of them that slew him.

Acts 23.9,11

⁹ And there arose a great cry: and the scribes that were of the Pharisees' part arose, and strove, saying, We find no evil in this man: but if a *spirit or an angel* hath spoken to him, let us not fight against God.

¹¹ And the night following the *Lord stood by him*, and said, Be of good cheer, Paul: for as thou hast testified of me in Jerusalem, so must thou bear witness also at Rome.

Acts 26.13-14

¹³ At midday, O king, I saw in the way a *light from heaven*, above the brightness of the sun, shining round about me and them which journeyed with me.

¹⁴ And when we were all fallen to the earth, I heard a *voice speaking* unto me, and saying in the Hebrew tongue, Saul, Saul, why persecute thou me? it is hard for thee to kick against the pricks.

Acts 27.23-25

²³ For there stood by me this night the *angel of God*, whose I am, and whom I serve,

²⁴ Saying, Fear not, Paul; thou must be brought before Caesar: and, lo, God hath given thee all them that sail with thee.

²⁵ Wherefore, sirs, be of good cheer: for I believe God, that it shall be even as it was told me.

Acts 28.3-6,9,25-31

³ And when Paul had gathered a bundle of sticks, and laid them on the fire, there came

a viper out of the heat, and fastened on his hand.

⁴ And when the barbarians saw the venomous beast hang on his hand, they said among themselves, No doubt this man is a murderer, whom, though he hath escaped the sea, yet vengeance suffers not to live.

⁵ And he *shook off the beast into the fire*, and *felt no harm.*

⁶ Howbeit they looked when he should have swollen, or fallen down dead suddenly: but after they had looked a great while, and saw no harm come to him, they changed their minds, and said that he was a god. And it came to pass, that the father of Publius lay sick of a fever and of a bloody flux: to whom Paul entered in, and prayed, and laid his hands on him, and healed him.

C.25 Here we can see a miracle of healing when normally getting a bite from that snake should have killed Paul.

⁸ And it came to pass, that the father of Publius lay sick of a fever and of a bloody flux: to whom Paul entered in, and prayed, and laid his hands on him, and *healed him*

⁹ So when this was done, others also, which had diseases in the island, came, and were *healed:*

²⁵ And when they agreed not among themselves, they departed, after that Paul had spoken one word, Well spake the Holy Ghost by Esaias the prophet unto our fathers,

²⁶ Saying, Go unto this people, and say, Hearing ye shall hear, and shall not understand; and seeing ye shall see, and not perceive:

²⁷ For the heart of this people is waxed gross, and their ears are dull of hearing, and their eyes have they closed; lest they should see with their eyes, and hear with their ears, and understand with their heart, and should be converted, and I should heal them.

²⁸ Be it known therefore unto you, that the salvation of God is sent unto the Gentiles, and that they will hear it.

²⁹ And when he had said these words, the Jews departed, and had great reasoning among themselves.

³⁰ And Paul dwelt two whole years in his own hired house, and received all that came in unto him,

³¹ Preaching the kingdom of God, and teaching those things which concern the Lord Jesus Christ, with all confidence, no man forbidding him.

C.26 The picture on the front cover of this book is for a reason as it shows Holy Spirit Mother embracing the world as She desires for many people to embrace Salvation in Her Son Jesus and for them to become anointed with Her the Holy Spirit Mother so that there can be 10s of thousands of witnesses or even millions of witnesses for Christ in these the End times. During the past 2000 years since the time of Jesus there have been many individuals and sometimes their followers who have set a very good example of what it means to be a true Christian.

C.27 Because of the world having descended into much darkness in recent years in every sense of the word, there needs to come *a great outpouring of God's Spirit* upon those who are the 'obedient of Christ' or the 'obedient of God' An expression used by Jethro in talking to Moses in the Old Testament. That example shows how God uses different peoples from many nations to proclaim the Truth. Jethro ended up giving very good advice to Moses, being his father- in -law.

C.28 I am very happy that there have been many honest people in the past years of darkness since Covid who have stood up against many of the evils and many who do proclaim Christ and Salvation from many denominations and non-denominations. We live in very interesting times, where we must watch out about the many lies of Satan and his many deceptions. We must look to the truth of God's Word as our anchor in life. We need Jesus to save us from our sins by His sacrifice on Calvary. His Mother the Holy Spirit is the one who helps us to proclaim the Truth both far and wide. Let's keep telling everyone about Jesus.

C.29 One does not have to be part of any particular church to know Jesus.

1st of all you need to acknowledge that you are a sinner and are in desperate need of Salvation to bring you to the light and God 'purpose in your life.

Please pray the following prayer to get saved in case you are not yet saved or tell others about this prayer if you already are saved:

SALVATION

Finally, I challenge you, that if you have not already prayed to receive Jesus into your heart, so that you can have eternal life, & be guaranteed an eternal place in Heaven, then please do so immediately, to keep you safe from what is soon coming upon the earth!

Revelations 3.20 "Behold, I stand at the door and knock, if any man hear my voice, and open the door, I will come in to him and live with him and him with me".

John 3.36 "He who believes on the Son of God has eternal life.".

That means right now! Once saved, you are eternally saved, and here is a very simple prayer to help you to get saved:

PRAYER

"Dear Jesus, please, come into my heart, forgive me all of my sins, give me eternal life, and fill me with your Holy Spirit. Please help me to love others and to read the Word of God in Jesus name, Amen."

Once you've prayed that little prayer sincerely, then you are guaranteed a wonderful future in Heaven for eternity with your creator and loved ones.

1 John 4.16 "For God is Love"

Your Salvation does not depend on you going to church, and your good works.

Titus 3.5 states "Not by works of righteousness which we have done, but according to His mercy he *saved* us".

Your salvation only depends on receiving Christ as your saviour, not on church or religion!

John 6.37 "He that comes unto Me, I will in no wise cast out"- Jesus

Jesus explained that unless you become as a child, you won't even understand the KINGDOM OF HEAVEN. **John 3.3**

CHAPTER 29: MILLENIUM -THE GOLDEN AGE

C.1 What a thought! Imagine a world with no more war. No more threat of nuclear war. No more bombs and weapons.

Beautiful Bible verses about the coming Millennium.

Isaiah 2:4 And he shall judge among the nations and shall rebuke many people: and they shall beat their swords into ploughshares, and their spears into pruninghooks: nation shall not lift up sword against nation, neither shall they learn war anymore.

Isaiah 9.6-7 For unto us a child is born, unto us a son is given: and the government shall be upon his shoulder: and his name shall be called Wonderful, Counsellor, The mighty God, The everlasting Father, The Prince of Peace.

C.2 Not like today when you turn on the TV and you don't know what to expect as wars are happening all the time and getting worse. Or some news about some horrible thing that man is doing somewhere on this planet to destroy it.

C.3 I wanted to explain that it is very important that everyone who claims to be a 'born again' Christian develops the gifts of the Spirit such as prayer and prophecy as well as having prophetic dreams upon occasion, allowing God to cause you to receive visions when necessary as well as to learn to hear directly from God As others have correctly stated: 'You should never do anything unless you get God's counsel first. Of course, it takes practice to develop these gifts of the Spirit of God the Mother. All these things were encouraged for the disciples to learn in the days of Paul the apostle. Having a love for God's Word is also essential.

Often it has been adversity and great difficulty which have caused God's people to develop these gifts. As in the case of missionaries in difficult circumstances.

C.4 'Eden Insights which is one of my books.' It is a book of brokenness and abandonment and yet happy re-union with God. This book is clearly showing how that Adam and Eve were very broken when they were kicked out of the Garden of Eden by God and they initially felt abandoned and totally lost and wondering where on earth they were -literally! God showed up more and more in their lives to show that He both loved them and was still very much with them.

C.3 Dreams: When you wake up you largely don't remember what you dreamed as the dream in general dissipates very quickly, or it just dissolves away, and you can't remember the dream at all. Personally speaking, when I have a dream whatever I was dreaming about whether good or bad interesting or not, the dream immediately fades away. It is as if I was an electrical devise that had suddenly been unplugged. Therefore, all that energy, knowledge, wisdom that I had gained during my dream is suddenly gone as it suddenly fades away.

Of course, those in heaven do not have this disadvantage as they are always close to God and His throne and are always plugged in to the light or Jesus and His precious Holy Spirit Mother and to God the Father. God has seen fit to do something to all of us when we sleep, that we are not fully conscious of. I am sure that we all have conversations with God and all kinds of communications do happen.

For the test of choice and this world, it has to all be 'unplugged' when we awake from our sleep. There are exceptions to that as I have pointed out. I have had some dreams that are indeed incredible, very vivid. Some dreams that came as soon as I put my head on the pillow.

C.4 My Dream of Sudden Attack: About one year ago, I had just put my head on the pillow when I found myself high up in the air and I could feel the winds against my face and suddenly this very large airplane flew right by me. It was descending at a very sharp angle, and I could see all the details of the aircraft. It looked like an old-fashioned large bomber with lots of windows and machine guns. It looked like the planes used in the 2nd World War or like the Dambusters.

During the 2nd world war, the idea was to get the planes to come down from height and fly very low skipping over the waves of the sea, in order to then go and blow up the dams in Germany during the 2nd World War.

The whole idea was to avoid being detected by radar by flying too low to be detected. I believe that dream was a warning that the *'powers that be'* were about to pull off a fast one, by using old fashioned tactics as were used during the 2nd World War some 80 years ago.

C.5 That was an exceptional dream that I actually remembered, and I immediately recorded it for future use. However, as I mentioned before, most of my dreams are simply not that significant.

When you sleep many things happen to you good and bad, most of which you simply are not allowed to remember. I think the reason that God hides most 'dream' occurrences from people in general is because if you had a fantastic experience up in heaven then why would you want to return to this crazy planet?!

Who in their right mind would want to come back here with the world in its current insane state? It is true. The more that you know and learn the more you wish that you didn't know. That is true in one sense but as has been said 'To foreknow is to be forearmed'.

C.6 I have also had **visions** in the **daytime** in broad daylight.

One year ago I had a revealing vision. Tragically the vision clearly showed me that both my brother and daughter would soon die that very year of 2024. Did it happen? Yes. My brother died only 5 days later, and our 34-year-old married daughter died 5 months later from cancer. That was a very vivid vision that I had in broad daylight whilst on my bicycle.[That exact vision was described on one of my Youtube videos @stephenstrutt]

Not everyone gets clear visions like this one, and I have only had a few but in very serious situations like the one just mentioned, you might be given a warning vision or dream. I have had quite a few visions and dreams of importance during my lifetime, but they are rare. It is important that we can all hear clearly from the spirit world. I think the reason why most of us don't remember some of our dreams is because if you had an amazing dream or spiritual experience up in heaven why would you want to return to this crazy planet in the morning as earth does not compare with heaven at the present time. The more you know, the more that you wish you didn't know, as others have said. That is correct in one sense, but it is also stated 'To know is to be forearmed'. For-armed for spiritual warfare. We are here to defeat Satan all the time with the Word of God.

C.7 SPIRITUAL EXPERIENCES

This morning, I had quite an experience in the Spirit. (6 months ago)

I was sitting down at my laptop going through the usual news in the world and on this particular occasion, I felt too tired to be bothered to read through the worldly news.

I had wanted to write something in this very book *Wisdom Insights* but felt that I just didn't feel well enough and that I was just too tired which I often feel these days although I am just 72 going on 73 -Still just a young sprout as some older people would say.

I sat on the sofa in our living room, but I didn't just want to lie down and rest, so I started reading one of my earlier books *'Eden Insights',* which is based on the Lost Books of Adam and Eve. I read the first few chapters, and I found it so inspiring, encouraging and informative.

Then I began to feel the Holy Spirit Mother come and encourage me -a sort of *warm fuzzy feeling like a small child with his wonderful loving Mother.* Her voice said to me 'Now that you are connected to us in heaven in prayer and the Word, 'Don't you want to go and write a few pages about me the Holy Spirit Mother in your new book of Wisdom Insights.

Immediately, I reacted, got up and said 'Of course I'll get to work right away'. And I did and wrote down these last pages about *Spiritual Happenings*.

C.8 I want to state that the Holy Spirit Mother is priceless, and you can get to know her by first of all getting saved by inviting Her Son Jesus the Messiah into your heart to cause you to be saved. Then the Holy Spirit Mother will take care of you as the Lord's child.

I went off immediately after being instructed and things were immediately flowing.

C.9 As a 'channel' myself 'things have got to be flowing' by the Spirit of God and not just me spouting off my own ideas. I am particularly interested in what God thinks of what I am writing. Is it true? Is it edifying? Is it helpful to others? I don't want to write just for the sake of writing. But to make sure that I am really saying something worthy of peoples' precious time.

C.10 I like to produce reading material that can feed other people's spirits and encourage their hearts and let them know that there is a God in our universe and that He truly cares for each one of us. He just wants us to learn to reach out to Him in prayer by the help of His precious Holy Spirit Mother and through their Son Jesus - the Word of God.

C.11 As I stated earlier, I think it important to read my book *Eden Insights* which is based on the *Lost Books of Adam and Eve.* That book shows how Adam and Eve suffered a lot especially in the very beginning or just after they were kicked out of the Garden of Eden.

They felt lost and abandoned for a while and they just couldn't believe that they had lost their contact with heaven-that is God, Jesus and all of heaven. It was almost too heart-breaking for them.

Wonderfully though, God did take great care of them and came to show them in person as LOGOS or Jesus the Word of God the Creator showed up in person to teach them all about their new existence and how to discern the evil of Satan and how to avoid him.

The Lost Books of Adam and Eve also show Satan doing a lot of sneaky attacks against Adam and Eve directly in person. Satan has from the beginning of Creation been totally bent on destroying mankind and God's Creation. Jesus told Adam and Eve in the beginning that they would not be allowed back into the Garden of Eden until He himself came to the earth and had given His life for all of mankind.

C.12 The Lost Books of Adam and Eve are fantastic in many ways and yet inspiring. Please get my book *'Eden Insights'* which includes both of those amazing Lost books of Adam and Eve. The 2nd Book of the 'Lost Books of Adam and Eve' shows the origin of the 'big fall of mankind' through Satan, evil and devils.

C.13 According to Hebrew scholars the main reason the Holy Spirit's gender was changed from feminine to masculine was when the Bible was translated from Hebrew into Greek and then into Latin. The pronouns are used differently in Greek and Latin. Well, that is how it started. I have covered this topic of the Holy Spirt being feminine in this book, and I do recommend that readers get a hold of the following other books by Marianne Widmalm – 'Our Mother the Holy Spirit' and Ally Kateusz' book -'Finding Holy Spirit Mother'.

C.14 In summary the Golden age of the future is one where not only the Lord Jesus and His saints rule over the nations and where Evil has been destroyed, but we will all learn to be creative in all of our thoughts and deeds as we also become creators. As has already been stated about heaven. It is a place where all your dreams do come true. God knows our hearts, and He knows what would make us the happiest. He cares about us and wants us to be eternally happy and fulfilled. We will be rewarded for all the good deeds that we have done for Christ and for love.

John 14.2-3

[2] In my Father's house are many mansions: if it were not so, I would have told you. I go to prepare a place for you.

[3] And if I go and prepare a place for you, I will come again and receive you unto

myself; that where I am, there ye may be also.

C.15 I will end this chapter with an amazing occurrence which happened to my wife and I and our granddaughter when my wife had just recently had a serious fall and concussion and was very ill indeed back in 2016.

Seraphim Bird visits our Garden

C.16 The other day on Wednesday 7th September 2016, my wife and I, had the privilege of being visited by a very beautiful Seraphim bird, which we found out later originated from the USA.

Whilst sitting in our garden, we had a beautiful experience, in seeing a rare bird arrive. We had never seen such a bird before, and though looking like a cross between a dove and pigeon, it had extremely feathered feet. My granddaughter quipped, that it looked like it had a rooster's feet.

The bird flew from our garage roof into the big tree in the centre of our small garden. It then flew onto one of the 2nd-floor windowsills. It appeared to be reasonably tame. It then finally went, and perched on the top windowsill to our bedroom, and promptly tucked its head in and went to sleep. Not surprising as to the timing as it had just started raining outside. We didn't have the heart to close the window, as long as this beautiful and gentle bird, was still perched on our windowsill, so we simply just left the window wide open all night. When we awoke the next morning, the beautiful bird was still there!

Then she awoke, and flew away, and we thought that was the last we would see this wonderful bird. But lo and behold, about half an hour later, the bird returned & flew right back onto our bedroom windowsill.

Our 7-year-old granddaughter, who happened to be visiting from Spain with our daughter, her mother, really enjoyed this adventure with this rare bird. We decided to call for expert attention, and we called Scotland's only charity for the preservation and protection of birds. They sent a young man who was obviously an expert with capturing escaped birds. He told us that it was very good that we had called them right away, as the bird was under-nourished. They promised to take good care of the bird and to re-house it with a good new bird-keeper.

We took the fact that my wife and family were visited by such a beautiful and rare bird as a very good Omen of Blessing, which is much appreciated by us at the present time, when my wife has been very ill for the past 10 months, due to a very severe concussion. I myself had also been very sick with severe anaemia at that time.

SERAPHIM

ISA.6:1 In the year that King Uzziah died, I saw the Lord sitting on a throne, high and lifted up, and the train of His robe filled the temple.

ISA.6:2 Above it stood seraphim; each one had six wings: with two he covered his face, with two he covered his feet, and with two he flew.

ISA.6:3 And one cried to another and said: 'Holy, holy, holy is the LORD of hosts;

The whole earth is full of His Glory!'

C.17 The word **Seraphim** (one seraph, two or more seraphim) They are also sometimes called the 'ones of love' because their name might come from the Hebrew root for 'love'. Seraphim are only fully described in the Bible on one occasion. This is in the book of the prophet Isaiah, when he is being commissioned by God to be a prophet and he has a vision of heaven.

C.18 In hindsight: We think that the above bird coming to visit us in 2016 was special indication from the Lord that I should start writing much more. I started my **INSIGHTS** books in 2017 or about 1 year after the above visit of the Seraphim Bird. Just a co-incidence? Or was it an encouragement about a new ministry of writing about God's Word.? I have now written 12 books, and this latest one is about the **Holy Spirit Mother** who is also depicted as a beautiful dove.

CHAPTER 30: EARLY CHRISTIAN FATHERS & HOLY SPIRIT MOTHER BY OTHER WRITERS

'The earliest Christians – all of whom were Jews – spoke of the Holy Spirit as a feminine figure. The present article discusses the main proof texts, ranging from the 'Gospel according to the Hebrews' to a number of testimonies from the second century. The ancient tradition was, in particular, kept alive in East and West Syria, up to and including the fourth century Makarios and/or Symeon, who even influenced 'modern' Protestants such as John Wesley and the Moravian leader Count von Zinzendorf. It is concluded that, in the image of the Holy Spirit as woman and mother, one may attain a better appreciation of the fullness of the Divine.'

For the Jewish Christians themselves, however, it was not merely a question of language. Apart from the *Gospel according to the Hebrews*, this is testified by a number of testimonies regarding the prophet Elxai. This Jewish Christian prophet—in the various sources also named as Elchasai, Alchasaios, Elkesai and Elxaios—is said to have received the revelation written about in the *Book of Elchasai* in Mesopotamia in the year 116–117.

The church father Epiphanius (c. 315–430), for many years bishop of Salamis and the metropolitan of Cyprus, transmits this revelation as follows:

Next he describes Christ as a kind of power and also gives His dimensions (...)And the Holy Spirit is (said to be) like Christ, too, but She is a female being (*thēleian*) (...). (Epiphanius, *Panarion* 19, 4, 1–2 –

Later on in his book, Epiphanius reports essentially the same:

And he [i.e., Elxai] supposed also that the Holy Spirit stands over against Him (i.e., Christ) in the shape of a female being (*en eidei thēleian*) (...). (Epiphanius, *Panarion* 30, 17, 6

The Pseudo-Clementines

A next testimony to the Holy Spirit's femininity may be derived from the so-called *Pseudo-Clementines*. The *Pseudo-Clementines* is a work circulated under the name of Clement of Rome (fl. c. 96), which came down to us in two fourth-century forms: the Greek *Homilies* and the Latin *Recognitions*. Both forms contain very old Jewish Christian source material. The Jewish Christian concept of the Spirit as a feminine Being is, by implication, preserved in one of the *Homilies*:

And Peter answered: 'One is He who said to His Wisdom, 'Let us make a man' [Gen. 1:26]. His Wisdom (*sophia*), with Her (Greek: *hei*, 3rd p. sing. feminine) He Himself always rejoiced [Prov. 8:30] just as (*hōsper*) with His own Spirit (*pneumati*).' (*Ps.-Clementines*, Hom. 16, 12, 1 –

The text identifies Wisdom with the Holy Spirit. This equation of Wisdom (*chokma, sophia*) and Holy Spirit (*ruach, pneuma*) has old parallels in Jewish and Jewish Christian traditions. Already in the Jewish book *Wisdom of Solomon*, preserved in Greek as part of the Septuagint and being in high esteem among most early Christian writers, one finds this equation; for instance, in *Wisdom* 9, 17 it runs:

Who has learned thy (i.e., God's) counsel, unless thou hast given wisdom (*sophian*) and sent thy holy Spirit (*pneuma*) from on high? (*Wisdom of Solomon* 9, 17 [Revised Standard Version])

Wisdom is equated with the Holy Spirit and both are considered to be feminine. Hence one understands how in early Christian tradition Christ is so often considered to be the child of mother Sophia or the Holy Spirit. In essence, both traditions express the same concept. The oldest patristic testimonies to this concept are the texts from Origen and Jerome quoted above.

In interpreting all these testimonies, one should bear in mind that ancient Jewish Christianity did not express itself in Greek discursive terminology, but in Semitic metaphorical language. Or, stated otherwise: the Jewish Christians expressed themselves in images, not in logical concepts. Accordingly, one may also understand that the Christian concept of Trinity is not merely due to Greek philosophical thinking, but has genuine and extremely old sources in Jewish Christian writings. One may reread the statements of Hippolytus and Epiphanius on Elxai's vision of God with his Son and the female Spirit as quoted above.

Theophilus and Irenaeus

The influence of the archaic Jewish Christian tradition on Spirit and Sophia is even found in Greek Christian authors such as Theophilus of Antioch (fl. later 2nd c.) and Irenaeus of Lyon (c. 130–c. 200). In his writing *Against Autolycus*, the Greek bishop and apologist Theophilus wrote for instance:

God made everything through His Logos and Sophia, for 'by His Logos the heavens were made firm and by His Spirit all their power.' [Ps.32:6] (...)

Similarly the three days prior to the luminaries [cf. Gn. 1] are types of the Triad (*triad*), of God and His Word and His Wisdom (Theophilus, *Ad Autol.* 1, 7; 2, 15

In Greek speaking bishop Irenaeus' work *Against Heresies*, which is mainly transmitted in Latin, it runs *inter alia*:

... the Son and the Holy Spirit (*Spiritus*), the Word and the Wisdom (*Sapientia*) (...)

For with Him were always present the Word and the Wisdom (*Sapientia*), the Son and the Spirit (*Spiritus*)

Irenaeus, *Adv. Haer.* 4, 7, 4; 20, 1.

The Pastor of Hermas

The *Shepherd of Hermas* is a rather enigmatic and, in all probability, composed document which originated in Rome between the end of the first and the middle of the second century. Its final form consists of five 'Visions', twelve 'Mandates' and ten 'Similitudes'. In the second and third centuries, it was accepted as Scripture by several ecclesiastical authors and even Didymus the Blind, a contemporary of Athanasius in the fourth century, included it in his canon of Scripture. It is also found in the highly important biblical manuscript Codex Sinaiticus, dating from the same time. In many of its utterances, the *Shepherd* reveals its Jewish Christian provenance.

One of these Jewish Christian features is the concept of the Holy Spirit as feminine. Although the *Shepherd of Hermas* (now generally classified as one of the 'Apostolic Fathers') uses the word 'spirit' in a variety of ways, in several cases 'spirit' appears to mean 'Holy Spirit'. One of these cases is *Similitude* IX, where the Holy Spirit is presented in the image of twelve virgins (*parthenoi*). The plural should not lead us astray here. Elsewhere in the *Shepherd* the Holy Spirit—in her equivalent the Church—is described as being pre-existent and also as an old women (*gunē presbutis*) (*Vis.* I, 2, 2; cf. e.g. II, 4, 1 ff.: *presbutera* in

Melito of Sardis

Some decades later, and in another part of the Roman Empire, Melito of Sardis († c. 190) composed his homily *On the Passover*. It became famous after its discovery and publication by Campbell Bonner in 1940. In its newest editions one finds some fragments added, the seventeenth of which reads as follows:

Hymn the Father, you holy ones; sing to your Mother (*tēi mētri*), virgins. We hymn, we exalt (them) exceedingly, we holy ones. You have been exalted to be brides and bridegrooms, for you have found your bridegroom, Christ. Drink for wine, brides and bridegrooms.

It does not seem to be beyond doubt that the fragment, which follows *On the Passover* in a Bodmer Papyrus Codex, really stems from Melito. In any case it is a liturgical dialogue, if not part from Melito's sermon, then perhaps of a baptismal liturgy. In its main theme and imagery, *On the Passover* is close to Jewish Christian thinking in general and Jewish Paschal tradition in particular. In the just quoted fragment, the Mother is without a doubt the Holy Spirit.

Sources from East and West Syria

As we have just seen with Theophilus, Irenaeus, the *Pastor Hermae* and (perhaps) Melito, the concept of the Spirit as feminine is sometimes found as an archaic reminiscence of Jewish Christianity in later Greek writers. However, in several Christian writings stemming from Syria, which mainly had Syriac (a branch of Aramaic) as their original language, this speaking of the Holy Spirit as feminine really abounds.

The Gospel of Thomas

Apart from some Greek scraps, the *Gospel of Thomas* has been mainly transmitted in a Coptic translation found in the second codex of the 'gnostic' library which, in December 1945, was discovered near Nag Hammadi in Upper Egypt. Many researchers maintain that the *Gospel of Thomas*—in any case in its original form(s)—was not 'gnostic' at all, nor even tincted with typical 'gnostic' ideas, but a fine example of primitive Jewish and Syrian Christianity. One of its *logia* reads as follows:

(Jesus said:) Whoever does not hate his father and his mother in My way will not be able to be a (disciple) to me. And whoever does (not) love (his father) and his mother in My way will not be able to be a (disciple) to me, for My mother (*tamaay*) (...) but (My) true (Mother) gave me the Life. (*Gospel of Thomas, logion* 101 – Guillaumont a.o. 1998:50;

Here, the true Mother is the Holy Spirit.

The Acts of Thomas

The *Acts of Thomas* recount the missionary activities of the apostle Judas Thomas. It is generally agreed that the composite work, which has survived in several Syriac and Greek manuscripts, was written in Syriac sometime before the middle of the third century. It contains many archaic elements pointing to early Jewish Christian tradition in Syria.

One of these archaic Jewish Christian elements is the concept of the Holy Spirit as feminine. It is clearly found in the following texts transmitted in Greek:

And the apostle arose and sealed them (...): Come, compassionate Mother (*mētēr*); (...) Come, Mother (*mētēr*) of the seven houses (...); Come, Holy Spirit (*pneuma*) and cleanse their loins and their heart, and seal them in the name of the Father and the Son and the Holy Spirit (*pneumatos*). (*Acta Thomae* 27

... we praise and glorify You (Christ), and Your invisible Father, and Your Holy Spirit (*pneuma*), (and) the Mother (*mētera*) of all creation. (*Acta Thomae* 39

Come, secret Mother (*mētēr*); Come, You who (*fem.*) are manifest in your deeds; You who (*fem.*) gives joy and rest to those who are united to You (*fem.*). (*Acta Thomae* 50

One may also compare *Acta Thomae* 7 (the Syriac text speaks of the glorification of 'the Father, the Lord of all' and 'the Spirit, His Wisdom') (cf. Klijn:29), whereas the Greek text has: 'The Father of truth and the Mother of Wisdom') and *Acta Thomae*133 ('We name over you [i.e. the 'bread of life' in the eucharist] the name of the Mother [= the Holy Spirit]).

hts.org.za/index.php/hts/article/view/3225/7763H

Gospels in Old Syriac, the Odes of Solomon, the Didascalia and the Apostolic Constitutions

A number of other writings from the Syrian world may be briefly dealt with under one heading. The first is the Old Syriac Version of the Gospels, which reaches back to the second century and transmits Jn 14:26 as follows:

... but that (Syr.: *hi* = she) Spirit, the Paraclete that my Father will send to you in my name, She (Syr. *hi*) shall teach you everything, She (*hi*) shall remind you of all what I say. (*Evangelium da-Mepharrese*

In all probability, the *Odes of Solomon* are a (Jewish) Christian work which is almost certainly written in Syria or Palestine in the course of the same second century. In *Ode* 36, 3 it runs:

The Spirit of the Lord rested upon me,

and She lifted me up to the height (...)

She brought me forth before the face of the Lord (...)

For according to the greatness of the Most High,

so She made me (...) (*Odes of Solomon* 36, 3a)

The *Didascalia Apostolorum* ('Teaching of the Apostles') is an ancient 'Church Order' which seems to have been composed in Syria in the earlier half of the third century. In the Syriac text of chapter 11 it runs:

This (i.e., the bishop) is your chief and your leader, and he is your mighty king. He rules in the place of the Almighty: but let him be honoured by you as God (...). But the deacon stands in the place of Christ, and do you love him. And the deaconess shall be honoured by you in the place of the Holy Spirit (...). (*Didascalia apostolorum* 9 –tr.

Virtually the same is stated in the *Apostolic Constitutions*, a collection of ecclesiastical commandments dating from the latter half of the fourth century and almost certainly of Syrian provenance:

Let also the deaconess (*diakonis*) be honoured by you in the place of the Holy Spirit (*eis typon tou hagiou pneumatos*) (...)

Aphrahat and Ephrem

Clear resonances of this kind of representation are present in Aphrahat. As a rule he is said to be the first of the (orthodox) Syriac church fathers and also 'the Persian sage'. We mainly know him from his so-called 'Demonstrations', a work dating from about 340. In the eighteenth *Demonstration* it runs with reference to Genesis 2:24:

Who is it that leaves father and mother to take a wife? The meaning is this. As long as a man has not taken a wife he loves and reveres God his Father and the Holy Spirit his Mother, and he has no other love.

One may add to this quote a passage from *Demonstration* VI, where Aphrahat speaks of the role of the Spirit in baptism:

From baptism we receive the Spirit of Christ, and in the same hour that the priests invoke the Spirit, She opens the heavens and descends, and hovers over the waters [cf. Gen. 1:2], and those who are baptized put Her on.

Although Ephrem Syrus (c. 306–373), who wrote most of his extant works in Edessa, conjugates the Syriac word *rucha* as feminine, one finds only one or two passages[9] in his œuvre which highlight her femininity. In one of these it runs:

It is not said of Eve that she was Adam's sister or his daughter, but that she came from him; likewise it is not to be said that the Spirit is a daughter or sister, but that (She) is from God and consubstantial with Him. (Ephrem, Commentary on the Concordant Gospel or Diatessaron 19, 15.

Makarios/Symeon

Finally, an extremely rich and influential source is constituted by the homilies of Symeon of Mesopotamia. For centuries, these homilies were transmitted under the name of Makarios (Macarius), an Egyptian monk who lived c. 300–390 and was a staunch supporter of Athanasius. Modern research, however, established that their real author is no other than a certain contemporary Symeon, who lived in Mesopotamia, in the vicinity of the upper Euphrates. The homilies of this Symeon mainly survive in Greek in four collections. The second collection, consisting of fifty 'spiritual' homilies, became the most popular, but the other three are important as well.

Here I quote only some of the most conspicuous examples, derived from a number of editions of the various collections. In the most influential *Fifty Homilies*, we read:

And from his (sc. Adam's) time until the last Adam, the Lord, man did not see the true heavenly Father and the good and kind Mother (*mētera*), the grace of the Spirit (*pneumatos*) (…). (Makarios/Symeon, *Hom.* 28, 4

Elsewhere it runs of the Holy Spirit:

She (*autē*) is the kind and heavenly Mother (*mētēr*) (…) (Makarios/Symeon, *Hom.* 27, 4)

Repeatedly it is stressed by Makarios that there is no human birth without a mother, and therefore no spiritual birth without the Holy Spirit (e.g. *Hom.* 8, 1;. As the mother (*mētēr*) of young birds cares for them, so the Holy Spirit provides food for God's children (*Hom.* 16, 2;. At another occasion, Makarios speaks of 'the grace of the Spirit, the Mother (*mētēr*) of the holy' (*Hom.* 27, 1;

Over the centuries, the writings of Makarios and/or Symeon have exerted an enormous influence, both in the East and in the West, not only in Syriac Christianity and other Eastern Orthodox circles, but also among Protestants. It is interesting to note that, among many others - both the very influential John Wesley and the also very influential Nikolaus Ludwig Graf von Zinzendorf were deeply influenced by Makarios. Although in the case of the first one I was not able to find any stress on the femininity of the Holy Spirit, in Zinzendorf there is indeed. In his first address in Pennsylvania, for instance, he said that 'the Father of our Lord Jesus Christ is our true Father, and the Spirit of Jesus Christ is our true Mother'.

It would be completely wrong to state that the image of the Holy Spirit as a woman and mother is simply caused by the fact that the Hebrew, Aramaic and Syriac words for 'spirit' are (nearly) always feminine. Of course this was an important factor, but there were other significant factors as well, such as the link between the figures of the Holy Spirit and Wisdom or between Holy Spirit and the Jewish feminine concept of the Divine Presence or Shekinah. Moreover, it should be remarked that, still, we are dealing with metaphorical language. Religious language is inherently metaphorical, that is, bound to images and similes. By its very nature it cannot define God's essence. All ancients were aware of the fact that this essence of the Divine remains a holy mystery and is by nature ineffable.

Nevertheless, the very first Christians, all of whom were Jews by birth, used to speak of the Holy Spirit as feminine. These Jewish Christians (or, perhaps better: Christian Jews) adhered to Genesis 1:27 where it is said that God created male *and* female after his image. If this text is really taken for true, then something female is inherent to God. Apart from the image of a Mother, Syrian and other Jewish Christians stressed the 'hovering' (*rahhef*) of the Spirit as stated, for instance, in Genesis 1:2 and Deuteronomy 32:11. Besides, they attributed to the Spirit the motherly features which Jewish prophetic writings like Isaiah (49:15–15; 66:13) find in God. One may also bring to mind that, according to Matthew, Jesus compared himself to a mother bird (Mt. 23:37). Moreover, when believers are born anew from the Spirit (e.g. Jn 3), they are 'children of the Spirit', who is their 'Mother'.

An expression such as 'children of the Spirit' is typical to Makarios. It explicitly refers to the motherly function of the Holy Spirit. There appears to be a tender aspect in God. **Is 66:13** which can only be expressed in the simile of the Mother. This does not mean that in this way we have 'defined' God; it just means that in this way we attain a better appreciation of the fullness of the Divine.' – Repeatedly it is stressed by Makarios that there is no human birth without a mother, and therefore no spiritual birth without the Holy Spirit As the mother (*mētēr*) of young birds cares for them, so the Holy Spirit provides food for God's children At another occasion, Makarios speaks of 'the grace of the Spirit, the Mother (*mētēr*) of the holy.'

Excerpt from: The Holy Spirit as feminine: Early Christian testimonies and their interpretation | van Oort | HTS Teologiese Studies / Theological Studies Epiphanius and Hippolytus on the prophet Elxai

Sirach amazes me still because **the entire book refers to Wisdom as She.** The Wisdom of Solomon and parts of Baruch do also, as well as Proverbs itself. Wisdom appears to be equivalent to the Spirit of God.

The earliest Christians – all of whom were Jews – spoke of the Holy Spirit as a feminine figure. The present article discusses the main proof texts, ranging from the 'Gospel according to the Hebrews' to a number of testimonies from the second century. The ancient tradition was, in particular, kept alive in East and West Syria, up to and including the fourth century Makarios and/or Symeon, who even influenced 'modern' Protestants such as John Wesley and the Moravian leader Count von Zinzendorf. It is concluded that, in the image of the Holy Spirit as woman and mother, one may attain a better appreciation of the fullness of the Divine.

Van Oort J., 2016, 'The Holy Spirit as feminine: early Christian testimonies and their interpretation', *HTS Teologiese Studies/Theological Studies* 72(1), a3225. http://dx.doi.org/10.4102/hts.v72i1.3225

The Maternal Face of the Holy Spirit

The Holy Trinity in St James Church, Upscaling

The most common image that depicts God as a mother can be found in Isaiah 42:14, where the prophet elaborates on Yahweh's anger and pain: "I have long time holden my peace; I have been still and refrained myself: now will I cry like a travailing woman; I will destroy and devour at once." In verse 16, he states that the world is reborn from God's labour pains: the darkness of the blind turns into light.

Moses complains about his people with the following words: "Of the Rock that begat thee thou art unmindful and hast forgotten God that formed thee."

(Deuteronomy 32:18).

The image of the woman in labour is also taken over by the New Testament: in Acts, in his Areopagus sermon, the Apostle Paul talks about God making references to Greek poets:

"For in him we live, and move, and have our being" (Acts 17:28). Apart from our time in our mother's womb, we never live *in* another person, but we can perhaps see the entirety of mankind – regardless of colour of skin, sex, religion, political and economic systems – living, moving and acting in the cosmic womb of God.

This view is reinforced by the Apostle Paul himself when he writes in his letter to the Romans: "For we know that the whole creation groans and travails in pain together until now. And not only they, but ourselves also, which have the first fruits of the Spirit, even we ourselves groan within ourselves, waiting for the adoption, to wit, the redemption of our body" (Romans 8:22-23). He seems to regard salvation as the birth, which happens not only in the lives of individual people, in the microcosm but in the entire creation, in the macrocosm.

In the Gospel of John, Jesus refers to the Holy Spirit as a mother: "That which is born of the flesh is flesh; and that which is born of the Spirit is spirit." (John 3:6). Being born from the flesh means being born from a human mother, while being born from the Spirit means being born from a divine mother. We will encounter this image in other passages as well.

These statements encourage us all to see the images of "being born again" as the evidence of the existence of the female component in the world, while the call for a spiritual rebirth should be interpreted as a call to experience God's maternal womb and mankind's birth from there. In other words, it is a call to quit our egotism and to tune into God's will the same way as the foetus is in complete harmony with and in the circulation of the mother carrying it. The discovery of God's motherhood could therefore serve not only our inner peace but also the universal peace of the human race.

APPENDIX I: GENETIC DISINTEGRATION

Genetic Entropy presents compelling scientific evidence that the genomes of all living creatures are slowly *degenerating* - due to the accumulation of slightly harmful mutations. This is happening despite natural selection. The author of this book, Dr. John Sanford, is a Cornell University geneticist. Dr. Sanford has devoted more than 10 years of his life to the study of this specific problem. Arguably, he has examined this problem in greater depth than any other scientist. The evidence that he presents are diverse and compelling. He begins by examining how random mutation and natural selection operate and shows that simple logic demands that genomes must degenerate. He then makes a historical examination of the relevant field (*population genetics*) and shows that the best scientists in that field have consistently acknowledged many of the fundamental problems he has uncovered (but they have failed to communicate these problems to the broader scientific community). He then shows, in collaboration with a team of other scientists, that state-of-the-art numerical simulation experiments consistently confirm the problem of genetic degeneration (even given very strong selection and optimal conditions). Lastly, in collaboration with other scientists, he shows that *real biological populations clearly manifest genetic degeneration.*

Dr. Sanford's findings have enormous implications. His work largely ***invalidates classic neo-Darwinian theory.*** The mutation/selection process by itself is not capable of creating the new biological information that is required for creating new life forms. Dr. Sanford shows that not only is mutation/selection incapable of creating our genomes - but it also can't even preserve our genomes. As biochemist Dr. Michael Behe of Lehigh University writes in his review of *Genetic Entropy*, "...not only does Darwinism not have answers for how information got into the genome, but it also doesn't even have answers for how it could remain there." Dr. Sanford has coined the term "genetic entropy" to describe this fatal flaw of neo-Darwinian theory. This fundamental problem has been something of a trade-secret within the field of population genetics, with the rest of the world largely being kept in the dark. Fortunately, this book finally discloses this very serious problem, using language that is for the most part accessible to all scholars and students having a basic understanding of biology. Get Dr Sanford's amazing insightful book on '**POPULATION GENETICS' AND 'GENE DE-GRADATION'**: https://answersingenesis.org/store/product/genetic-entropy-mystery-genome/?sku=10-3-114

APPENDIX II: GEO-CENTRIC UNIVERSE

Here is a very interesting article about Creation which shows a Geo-Centric view of our universe, or the fact that the sun rotates around the earth and not Helio-central that the earth rotates around the sun. This article also mentioned pregnancies in the Bible and their great significance concerning Creation itself.

The *Book of Enoch* would also seem to support a geocentric view of the universe in chapters *72-75*, under the heading "The Book of the Courses of the Heavenly Luminaries".

"And I saw six portals in which the sun rises, and six portals in which the sun sets and the moon rises and sets in these portals, and the leaders of the stars and those whom they lead: six in the east and six in the west, and all following each other in accurately corresponding order: also many windows to the right and left of these portals." *-Enoch 72:3*

Below are some verses related to the subject matter. All the Old Testament verses come from the Septuagint version of the Bible. The New Testament verses are from the King James Version.

Joshua said,

Let the sun stand over against Gabaon, and the moon over against the valley of Alon. And the sun and the moon stood still, until God executed vengeance on their enemies; and the sun stood still in the midst of heaven; it did not proceed to set till the end of one day.

Joshua 10:12-13

The sun was exalted, and the moon stood still in her course.

Habakkuk 3:11

Their voice is gone out into all the earth, and their words to the ends of the world. In the sun he has set his tabernacle; and he comes forth as a bridegroom out of his chamber: he will exult as a giant to run his course. His going forth is from the extremity of heaven, and his circuit to the other end of heaven.

Psalm 19:4-6

The sun arises, and the sun goes down and draws toward its place; arising there it proceeds southward, and goes round toward the north.

Ecclesiastes 1:5

Let the whole earth fear before him; let the earth be established, and not be moved. 1

Chronicles 16:30

The Lord reigns; he has clothed himself with honour: the Lord has clothed and girded himself with strength; for he has established the world, which shall not be moved.

Psalm 93:1

Say among the heathen, The Lord reigns: for he has established the world so that it shall not be moved.

Psalm 96:10 It is he that comprehends the circle of the earth.

Isaiah 40:22 It is he that sits upon the circle of the earth, and the inhabitants thereof are as grasshoppers; that stretches out the heavens as a curtain, and spreads them out as a tent to dwell in:

GEO-CENTRIC UNIVERSE From: Galileo Was Wrong The Church Was Right

The Evidence from Modern Science

by Robert A. Sungenis, Ph.D. And Robert J. Bennett, Ph.D. Galileo Was Wrong: The Church Was Right: The Evidence from Modern Science, Volume II, 11th Edition (Galileo Was Wrong: The Church Was Right - The Evidence from Modern Science & Church History Book 2) eBook : Sungenis, Robert, Bennett, Robert : Amazon.co.uk: Kindle Store

APPENDIX III: TIME-FRAME OF 7000 YEARS OF WORLD HISTORY

(Approximate dates AC=After Creation)

CREATION	AC 0 (±4000 BCE)
ENOCH	AC 600
NOAH	AC 1000
ABRAHAM	AC 2000
MOSES	AC 2500
DAVID	AC 3000
DANIEL	AC 3500
JESUS CHRIST	AC 4000
DARK AGES AC	5000
MODERN TIMES	AC 6000
2ND COMING OF CHRIST circa	AC 6000
MILLENIUM	AC 6000-7000
GREAT WHITE THRONE JUDGEMENT	AC 7000
THE NEW HEAVEN & THE NEW EARTH	AC 7000 to ETERNITY

APPENDIX IV: SALVATION

Finally, I challenge you, that if you have not already prayed to receive Jesus into your heart, so that you can have eternal life, & be guaranteed an eternal place in Heaven, then please do so immediately, to keep you safe from what is soon coming upon the earth!

Revelations 3.20 "Behold, I stand at the door and knock, if any man hear my voice, and open the door, I will come in to him and live with him and him with me".

John 3.36 "He who believes on the Son of God has eternal life.".

That means right now! Once saved, you are eternally saved, and here is a very simple prayer to help you to get saved:

PRAYER

"Dear Jesus, please, come into my heart, forgive me all of my sins, give me eternal life, and fill me with your Holy Spirit. Please help me to love others and to read the Word of God in Jesus name, Amen."

Once you've prayed that little prayer sincerely, then you are guaranteed a wonderful future in Heaven for eternity with your creator and loved ones.

1 John 4.16 "For God is Love"

Your Salvation does not depend on you going to church, and your good works.

Titus 3.5 states "Not by works of righteousness which we have done, but according to His mercy he *saved* us".

Your salvation only depends on receiving Christ as your saviour, not on church or religion!

John 6.37 "He that comes unto Me, I will in no wise cast out"- Jesus

Jesus explained that unless you become as a child, you won't even understand the KINGDOM OF HEAVEN. **John 3.3**

APPENDIX V: BOOKS

HERE ARE MY 12 BOOKS WITH ME BEING INTERVIEWED ABOUT THEM: 10 OF THE 12 BOOKS ARE 'INSIGHTS BOOKS' WHICH ARE BASED ON ANCIENT HEBREW BOOKS AND APOCRYPHAL BOOKS.

1) ENOCH INSIGHTS : https://www.youtube.com/watch?v=yB5jE6CO350&t=1150s

2) EZDRAS INSIGHTS : https://www.youtube.com/watch?v=6qGN5HLArGo

3) JASHER INSIGHTS BOOK 1. https://www.youtube.com/watch?v=yjoKYs1JpI4&t=2060s

4) JASHER INSIGHTS BOOK 2. https://www.youtube.com/watch?v=yjoKYs1JpI4&t=2060s

5) JUBILEES INSIGHTS. https://www.youtube.com/watch?v=LDY9T75bGiE&t=90s

6) EDEN INSIGHTS: https://www.youtube.com/watch?v=0lgCYrcQ_58

7) TESTAMENTS OF THE TWELVE PATRIARCHS 'INSIGHTS.: https://www.youtube.com/watch?v=wgqsyggVwX

8) ESDRAS INSIGHTS
https://www.youtube.com/watch?v=6qGN5HLArGo

9) 10) & 11) BOOKS ON THE PARANORMAL: OUT OF THE BOTTOMLESS PIT BOOKS 1 & 2: https://www.youtube.com/watch?v=coQN93sRffM

11) SECRETS OF ENOCH INSIGHTS: https://www.youtube.com/watch?v=aEL_JNs7Oto&t=973s

12) WISDOM INSIGHTS 'HOLY SPIRIT MOTHER''THE QUEEN OF HEAVEN' *'INSIGHTS'*

(116) Holy Spirit Mother – Is the Holy Spirit Female? – with Stephen Strutt - YouTube

AVAILABLE AT AMAZON, 'BARNES AND NOBLE' IN THE USA - OR WATERSTONES IN THE UK - OR DIRECTLY FROM ME AT: insightsbooks@gmail.com

My new website which is made to illustrate my 12 books:
www.insightspublication.com